About the Author

Dr. Robert A. Morey is the author of over 60 books, some of which have been translated into French, German, Italian, Dutch, Danish, Swedish, Spanish, Arabic, Farsi, Polish, and Finnish. He is listed in *The International Authors* and *Writers Who's Who and Contemporary Authors*.

Education

He has earned the following degrees:

Date	Degree	Institution
1969	B.A. (Philosophy)	Covenant College
1972	M.Div. (Theology)	Westminster Theological Seminary
1989	D.Min. (Apologetics)	Westminster Theological Seminary
1996	D.D. (Honorary)	Faith Theological Seminary
2004	PhD. (Islamic Studies)	Louisiana Baptist University
2005	Culinary Arts (Chef)	Thompson Institute

Professional Training

Dr. Morey was the Chairman of the Membership Committee of the Evangelical Theological Society for several years. Dr. Morey is recognized internationally as a professional apologist and theologian whose careful scholarship and apologetic abilities establish him as one of Christianity's top defenders. He was also adjunct Professor of Apologetics at Evangelical Theological Seminary and founder and past President of California Biblical University and Seminary (CBUS). He has studied alongside some great Christian theologians and apologists. They include: Walter Martin (NYC, NJ CRI), Francis Schaeffer (Covenant College, L'Abri in Switzerland) Gordon Clark, (Covenant College) Cornelius Van Til (WTS), and Hans Rookmaaker (NYC, Holland L'Abri).

Ministry Involvement (Past and Present)

- Adjunct professor at various seminaries
- Lectured at seminaries, universities, colleges, and churches in 27 countries
- Appeared on hundreds of radio and TV programs such as 700 Club, Coral Ridge Ministry, TBN, John Ankerberg Show, Moody Network, etc.
- Host of his own national talk show: *Bob Morey Live!*
- Executive Director of Faith Defenders (1984-2014)
- Founder and Past President of California Biblical University and Seminary (CBUS)
- Pastor of New Life Bible Church 1977-1998
- Pastor of Faith Community Church 2005-2008

RECOMMENDATIONS FOR DR. MOREY'S MINISTRY

Dr. Morey's speaking and writing ministry is recommended by some of the best-known Christian leaders in this generation.

Dr. D. James Kennedy (Coral Ridge Ministries)
"Dr. Robert A. Morey is an excellent speaker and writer on the subjects of cults and the occult. His books are excellent resource tools on these subjects. It is my pleasure to recommend him to churches everywhere throughout our land."

Dr. John Ankerberg (The Ankerberg TV Show)
"I have known Dr. Robert Morey for a number of years and welcome this opportunity to recommend him to you. Dr. Morey is a man with an excellent understanding of the historic Christian faith and a particular skill as a defender of the Faith. I heartily recommend him to you."

Dr. Stephen Olford (Dr. Morey's pastor for eight years)
"I praise the Lord that He has given you such a strategic ministry in the field of apologetics and theology. The Lord bless you richly."

Dr. Herbert Ehrenstein (Editor of Eternity Magazine)
"It is a genuine privilege for me to recommend Dr. Robert A. Morey as a competent Biblical scholar in the field of apologetics, Bible teaching and evangelism. I have known Dr. Morey for over 30 years and it has been a delight to me to see his developing a fantastic grasp of Biblical truth, and his unique ability to translate that exalted truth of God's Word into down-to-earth, meaningful and methodical ways his audiences can make use of it."

Dr. Kevin Johnson (Mount Carmel Outreach)
"Dr. Robert Morey is one of the finest Biblical scholars in the field of comparative religious studies (apologetics) in North America.

His books and presentations have been tremendously useful. I highly recommend him to you."

RECOMMENDATIONS FOR THIS BOOK

"Dr. Morey's translation of the Book of Psalms is a good way to know the sense of the Hebrew poetry in its freshness to see the soul of it is clearly written so that you feel the passion of the spirituality throbbing in the Psalms. The Bible student as well as pastors will rejoice in this book. I recommend this awe-inspiring translation to anyone who wants to understand the Psalms."

Bishop Colin P. Akridge
Professor and Army Veteran.

"This is the God-centered, Christ-exalting, game changing translation of the Psalms that serious students of the Bible have been waiting for. It brings out the beauty of the Hebrew text as well as the original intent of the Author in a groundbreaking way."

Dr. Brian James Shanley
Sovereign Grace Institute of Apologetics

"Dr. Morey's translation brings the Psalms to life like No other translation. Not only does he explain the Psalms as songs of worship but he also he explains how they relate to day by day life. I wish I had this translation 45 years ago when I started preaching. I recommend this uplifting translation to any Bible student, Bible College professor or seminary professor, and pastor. It has been a delightful experience reading it. I could almost hear the musical instruments playing and choirs singing. This translation will change your life!"

Rev. Dr. Charles Christopher (B.A., M.Div., D.M.)

Dedication

I dedicate this translation to the godly women who inspired me to live for the Lord. Anne Morey, my beloved wife of forty years. She was my best friend, lover, ministry partner, and dedicated mother of our children. Ruth Morey (my grandmother), Delia Varene, Edith Schaeffer, Granny Cowan, Johanna Michaelsen, Corrie ten Boom, Mary Shum, Colette Grady, Dorothy Epperley, Rosemary Miller, Ruth Woerz, Rodina MacLean, Pat Shenk, Joy Nacionales, and Nadine Veltman.

"The Sovereign Lord gave the Word and numerous were the women who proclaimed it." (Psa. 68:11).

TABLE OF CONTENTS

About the Author i

Recommendations for Dr. Morey's Ministry iii

Dedication vi

Authors preface viii

Introduction x

Forward: Experiencing God in the Psalms xii

Introduction: The Pentateuch of the Psalms 1

A Well Known Cluster of Psalms 4

Book I (Psalms 1-41) 11

Book II (Psalms 42-72) 109

Book III (Psalms 73-89) 182

Book IV (Psalms 90-106) 230

Book V (Psalms 107-150) 271

Appendix A: Philosophy of Translation 353

Appendix B: The Meaning of Sheol 358

Footnotes 373

Author's Preface

What is the purpose of the Psalms? Why did God inspire them and include them in the canon of Scripture? What is the goal that we should have in mind as we read them?

The first thing to understand is that in the Bible God speaks to us as individuals, families, churches, and nation. In the Psalms God addresses us as individuals.

God speaks to us in Scripture because He wants us to know something (knowledge acquisition), to be something (character development) or to do something (call to action). The Psalms are a call to action. As you read the Psalms you are to do something in response.

The Psalms were written to usher you into the realized presence of God; to enable you to ascend to heaven and join the holy angels in worship and praise. The Psalms call upon you to experience the realized presence of God.

In this sense, the Psalms must be *experienced* in order to be understood. Thus, do not passively read the Psalms in a cold, sterile, academic manner. Do look at them objectively from the outside but subjectively enter inside and experience them.

This is why unbelievers cannot understand the Psalms.

An unregenerate person does not accept the things of the Spirit of God, for they are foolishness to him; he cannot understand them, because they are spiritually discerned. (1 Cor. 2:14)

In order to understand the Psalms you have to experience them by praying them, singing them, worshipping God through them, feeling their power, following the flow of the mind of the Psalmist all the way to the throne of God.

Entering the very presence of God is the purpose, function, and goal of the Psalms. Anything less is abject failure. To the degree you experience God through the Psalms is the degree to which you really understand them.

In order to enhance the experiential nature of the Psalms, several things had to be done. First, I needed to produce a new dynamic translation of the Psalms from the Hebrew text.

I must give special thanks to the International Standard Version for choosing me to be part of the translation team for the Psalms. They also gave me permission to use the ISV Psalms as the jumping off point for my own new translation.

For my philosophy of translation, see Appendix A. I also add a discussion of the Hebrew sheol in Appendix B.

Introduction

Christians today are just beginning to rediscover their Jewish roots. When Edith Schaeffer wrote the book, *Christianity is Jewish*, back in 1977, most Christians did not have a clue as to what she was saying.

Francis and Edith Schaeffer at L'Abri were ahead of the curve in this regard. They took special joy in teaching new Jewish believers that they were now "completed" Jews who had embraced their Jewish Messiah. They did not betray Judaism by accepting Yeshua (Jesus). They were the *true* Israel who worshipped the triune God of Israel. Gentiles who accepted the Jewish Messiah as their Savior were now grafted into Spiritual Israel (Rom. 11:17f).

My wife and I learned these important truths while at L'Abri in 1972 and later introduced Messianic worship in every church we pastored for 40 years.

In the 1970s and 1980s we took our Gentile Christian friends to Messianic conferences where they learned to dance and sing in praise of God. Our church worship services were filled with JOY and not the typical dead church service most Christians endure today.

At the beginning we were looked upon as "odd" by traditional churches who could not understand our love of Jewish things. I often began the worship service with the "Shamah." I am happy to report that in the last twenty five years, Messianic songs, dancing, and worship have been adopted by many Gentile congregations.

We must remember that the *only* reference in the New Covenant Jewish Scriptures (mistakenly called the "New Testament") to the building where Christians met to worship was "synagogue" (James 2:2). Let the readers take note to the reference to the synagogue building in James 2:2. Your "church" is actually a messianic synagogue. For more details on the Jewish nature of Christianity, see my books on the relationship between the Old and New testaments, and the structure of the Bible.

Elements of Jewish worship are now part of many public worship services: clapping, antiphonal singing, dancing, waving flags, use of stringed instruments such as the harp, even sounding the shofar can now be heard in churches all over the world. See my book, *Worship: It's Not Just Sunday Morning*.

As Gentile Christians have grown in their appreciation of their Jewish spiritual roots, they have begun rethinking the role of the Psalms in public worship. The singing of the Psalms had fallen into disrepute because of the false teaching of Exclusive Psalmody. Since I refuted this false teaching in *The Encyclopedia of Practical Christianity*, we will not refute it again in this book.

In the early 1970s, we introduced the singing of the Psalms in our churches and have since rejoiced to see many churches discovering the truth of General Psalmody: God inspired a hymnal for the church as well as for the temple and synagogue. We have Psalms, hymns, and spiritual songs in the five books of the Psalms that should be incorporated into the public and private worship of all Christians, Gentile or Jewish. They also serve as a pattern for us to produce new Psalms, hymns, and spiritual song in our own day.

With these few brief words, it is our great joy and honor to publish a new translation of the Psalms from the original Hebrew text along with insights gained from the Greek, Aramaic, and Latin translations, and from the Talmuds, Mishnahs, Midrash, Targums, and Dead Sea Scrolls. The use of rabbinic sources is sometimes necessary for the historical background of the Psalms.

FOREWARD
by Pastor Randolph C. Michaelsen

Experiencing God in the Psalms

For millennia, people have turned to the Psalms for comfort and strength in times of sorrow. Even those only marginally acquainted with the God of the Bible sometimes find themselves thumbing through the Psalms seeking a word of encouragement and hope. The faithful have long looked to the Psalms to give a holy voice to their praise and exultation of the Living God, finding in them an expression of their trust in His sovereign goodness and faithfulness. How often have God's people opened that book of matchless poetry simply to remember His wonderful works and meditate on the beauty of His Holiness!

The Psalms are God's own Hymn Book written for us by the Spirit of God. By the breath of the Spirit of God we are born again and through faith in Jesus Christ are given the right to become children of God. By that same breath, out of the very heart of God, are born hymns and spiritual songs to inform and encourage true worship; Psalms that draw us into the very presence and experience of God. How wonderful to have songs to remind us that there is no place so remote, so hidden, so dark and seemingly hopeless that He does not see, that He does not hear, to which He cannot bring His presence.

The inspired writings of the Prophets and Apostles are sprinkled everywhere with quotes and echoes from the Psalms. From Jonah in the belly of the great fish to Peter on the Day of Pentecost; from Jeremiah and Ezekiel and Isaiah to the last chapter of the Apostle John's Revelation, the Holy Spirit repeatedly points us back to the Psalms. Even as He hung on the cross, the words of Psalm 22 were among the last uttered by our Lord Jesus: "My God, my God, why have You forsaken me?"

With God is the fountain of life and He invites us daily to drink from the wells and streams of salvation for refreshing and renewal. There is a flow from heaven that God has provided to strengthen and encourage us. But even beyond that, God longs to draw us into His very Presence to fellowship with Him. Those who yearn to experience the true presence of God need not look to Eastern occult techniques or meaningless repetitions which produce only a counterfeit shadow and mockery of true fellowship with God. Look to the Psalms to draw you into a genuine encounter with the Living God!

Dr. Morey's new translation of the Psalms seeks to return them to the form and intent of original language in which they were written. He has daringly removed the superimposed verse divisions and poetic forms of sixteenth-century England, in order to bring us dynamic new insights of the Psalms as they were originally meant to be read and experienced. You will find yourself enabled to follow the heart and mind of the authors of the Psalms with a refreshing clarity.

May your faith be strengthened and your heart filled with joy, as you immerse yourself in this wonderful work! Pastors, in particular, should find this an invaluable tool in their preaching.

Pastor Randolph C. Michaelsen
Pastor of Prayer/Visitation Ministry
Kings Harbor Church

Johanna Michaelsen
Author/Lecturer

Introduction

The Pentateuch of the Psalms

If I had a dollar for every time Christians have told me that they did not know that the Psalms were divided into five distinct scrolls (books) and not just one book I could retire to Belize!

Many modern translations delete Book One, Book Two, Book Three, Book Four, and Book Five in the heading of the Psalms. On what grounds did they drop these titles when they are in the Hebrew, Greek and Latin versions? None whatsoever! The translators were totally ignorant of their importance and function in the interpretation of the Psalms.

If you examine the version of the Bible you generally use and do not see "Book One" above Psalm One, etc. you are dealing with a false translation. Replace it with a translation that has the Psalms divided into Five Books.

The five books that make up the Psalms are a Pentateuch just like the five books of Moses are a Pentateuch. Just as Moses' Pentateuch gives us the Torah of earthly laws, the Pentateuch of the Psalms gives us the Torah of heavenly laws. Moses' Torah deals with the visible while the Psalms' Torah deals with the invisible. They instruct us in important lessons for living a righteous life.

The Pentateuch of the Psalms reveals universal, spiritual principles or rules that can be applied by everyone in every generation and in every culture. These principles are not culturally bound or temporally limited to ancient Israel. This is why we can use the Psalms in prayer, praise and worship today.

The Order of the 150 Psalms

I usually take hundreds of 3x5 cards up to the pulpit or lectern as visual aids. I begin by asking, "How many Christian songs are floating around these days?" I answer, "Thousands!!! Multiple thousands! How many songs existed in ancient Israel? Thousands!"

Why?

Singing has always been part of the worship of God because man was created in the image of the Great Musician who is the Origin of music. The angels sang at the Creation, the Seraphim sing in heaven, and even the Messiah is described as the "singing" Messiah (Job 38:7; Isa. 6:3; Psa. 22:22 cf. Heb. 2:12).

In ancient Israel, there were thousands of worship "Psalms, hymns, and spiritual songs" arranged as instrumental music, solos, choir music, personal prayers, and testimonies.

Worship Medium	Definition	Example Psalm
Psalms	Musical compositions that featured various musical instruments such as the eight-string lyre.	6
Hymns	Celebrated God's mighty deeds in the history of redemption.	78
Spiritual Songs	Personal testimonies and prayers for what God has done in your life.	138

I take the stack of hundreds of cards and set aside all but 150 cards. I then state,

"God inspired these 150 'Psalms, hymns, and spiritual songs' to be used in private, family, and public worship. Since He is a God of order and not chaos, it should not surprise you to find that the order of the 'Psalms, hymns, and spiritual songs' manifests intelligent design that communicates information of a high order that far exceeds human ingenuity."

I then ask, "Are these 150 'Psalms, hymns, and spiritual songs' organized in any way?" Sorry to say, not once in forty years has a single student or congregation known the answer. The "Psalms, hymns, and spiritual songs" are divided into five scrolls (mistranslated as "Books" by the KJV).

Scroll #	Chapters
1	1-41
2	42-72
3	73-89
4	90-106
5	107-150

I then take the stack of 150 cards and divide them into five piles. I then ask,

"Do you think that God is smart enough to know which scroll contains which Psalms or did He just throw them up into the air and let them fall into five piles by chance? No! Each Psalm was placed on a specific scroll by Divine Wisdom. Is God really smart enough to have specific reasons for putting a specific Psalm on a specific scroll? Of course! Having gone to the trouble of deciding which Psalm goes on which scroll, do you think He put those Psalms into a specific order that conveys intelligent information to the readers? Yes."

I love working with seminary students, especially when they ask intelligent questions. During one lecture on the meaning of the order of the Psalms, a student raised his hand to challenge me. He said, "How do you know that the Jews had the same Psalms we have and that they were in the same order as we have in our Bible?" Good question. I had him turn to Acts 13:33 and

read it out loud. When he saw the words "written in the second Psalm," he had an "epiphany" of knowledge. I asked him, "Is the 2nd Psalm Paul referred to the same 2nd Psalm we find in our Bible?"
Yes!

A Well-Known Cluster of Psalms

Most pastors at some point have noticed the phrase "Songs of Ascents" (NASV) or "Songs of Degrees" (KJV). They are part of the titles from Psa. 120 to Psa. 134. These fifteen Psalms are obviously grouped together to give us Intelligent information about them. A proper interpretation of these Psalms must take into account which scroll they are on, their place in that scroll, and the order in which they are placed. They are like 15 different musical instruments in a symphony playing a Bach Fugue.

Preachers must observe the order in which each Psalm was placed and notice if it is part of a cluster of Psalms. In this case, the rabbinic understanding of these fifteen "Psalm of Ascents" is explained by the *International Standard Bible Encyclopedia*:

> According to the Mishna, Middoth 2 5, Cukkah 51b, there was in the temple a semi-circular flight of stairs with 15 steps which led from the court of the men of Israel down to the court of the women. Upon these stairs the Levites played on musical instruments on the evening of the first day of Tabernacles. Later Jewish writers say that the 15 Psalms derived their title from the 15 steps.

While the "Songs of Ascent" are obviously a meaningful arrangement of Psalms, there are many other clusters as well. But they require the interpreter to think about how each Psalm relates to the Psalm before and the Psalm after it.

Going Deeper

Psalms 22, 23 and 24 is another example of how the Psalms are arranged in such a way as to convey information of the highest order.

Prophet, Priest, and King

The three offices of prophet, priest, and king under the Old Covenant were always kept separate and distinct. If you held one of the three offices, you were not allowed to invade the other two offices. For example, when King Uzziah tried to usurp the priesthood by offering a sacrifice, he was struck down with leprosy (2 Chron. 26:16-21). No one, not even the king, could usurp other offices.

The Three Offices of Messiah

While this was true of normal man, when the divine Messiah came, He would hold all three offices of prophet, priest, and king at the same time. This is why the great creeds of the Church describe the work of Jesus Christ as prophet, priest, and king.

I have the audience turn to Psa. 22 and tell them to draw a cross next to the title. Then they should write the words "Priest," "Jesus" and "Savior" next to the cross. Why? Psa. 22 is the "crucifixion Psalm" cited by Matthew as predicting the betrayal, arrest, trial, and death of Messiah (Matt. 26-27).

In Psa. 22 the Messiah is predicted as the Priest who would offer up himself on the cross as the sacrifice to make atonement for the people of God. See my book *Studies in the Atonement* for the details.

In the New Testament the Messiah was given the name "Jesus" because he would be the "Savior" of His people (Matt. 1:21). As a homework assignment, go through Psa. 22 and identify each verse that is cited by Matthew as a prophecy about Jesus.

The Son of God was not only called "Jesus" but also "Christ," i.e. the anointed prophet of God. Just as Psa. 22 focuses on the priesthood of Messiah, Psa. 23 focuses on the prophet-hood of Messiah.

I tell people to draw a shepherd's crook next to the title of Psa. 23 and then write the words "Prophet," "Christ," and "Sanctifier" next to it. The Son of God is Savior (Psa. 22) and Shepherd (Psa. 23).

Psa. 24 focuses on the Kingship of Messiah. Draw a crown next to the title and write the words "King," "YHWH," and "Sovereign" next to it. Jesus is Savior, Shepherd, and Sovereign because He is priest, prophet, and king.

As our High Priest, Jesus gave the ultimate sacrifice of Himself on the cross to atone for our sins. As our Prophet, He guides us throughout our pilgrimage on earth. As our King, He provides for us, protects us from our enemies, and has secured the ultimate victory for us over hell and the grave. What a Messiah!

Meditate on the Word

God calls upon us to *meditate* on His Word (ex. Josh 1:8; Ps 1:2; 63:6; Isa 33:18). This requires peace and quiet and the time to think deeply about the meaning of words, sentences, paragraphs, chapters, Psalms, etc. It means to check good commentaries on the passage.

"Preaching" the Word is easy. Anyone with the gift of gab can get up and waste everyone's time by giving his own personal opinion. But preaching the Word of God *correctly* requires you to *"labor* in the Word and doctrine" (1 Tim. 5:17). The pulpit is no place for lazy men.

If you are a pastor reading this book, we wrote it to help you, not complicate your life with unnecessary burdens. The New Covenant Jewish Scriptures (i. e. the New Testament), requires pastors to "labor in the Word" (1 Tim. 5:18). The Greek word translated "labor" means hard back-breaking work. It takes WORK to labor in the Word and in Doctrine.

The Psalms as Torah

The five books of the Psalms focus on living in the light of God's "Torah" (i.e. Torah) because they reveal God's principles, rules or

Torahs for all of life. The Torah encompasses all of life and is not just about "soul-saving" or "pie in the sky, by and by."

YHWH establishes at the beginning of human history that He is YHWH of ALL of life. There is no secular/sacred dichotomy in the Bible because all of life is sacred and under the Lordship of YHWH.

God Is the Origin of All Things

The Pentateuch establishes at the dawn of human history that the Origin and Author of truth, justice, morals, meaning, and beauty is God alone. Man, beginning only with himself, cannot be the Origin of these things. Man *qua* man was never created to create truth and morals but to receive them via special revelation from the God who created man. For further discussion of this reality, see my book, *The Bible, Natural Theology and Natural Law: Conflict or Compromise?*

The Psalms Are for All Christians

The Psalms are for all who believe in Jesus the Messiah. Read them, sing them, pray them, and use them in worship. They will enrich every area of your life.

Musical Compositions

Most of the Psalms are musical compositions intended for solos, duets, choirs, antiphonal singing, and instrumental music for orchestras. Sometimes the Psalmist even states the musical instruments he wants to be used.

Psalm 150 is a beautiful example of the musical nature of the Psalms. It is the musical climax of all the Psalms, hymns, and spiritual songs. It is last because it brings you into the worship of God with full choir and orchestra.

As you enter the temple, you see the mass choir assembled, the entire orchestra in front of the singers, and the dancers with tambourines off to the sides.
The choir director, dressed in his finest robes, is also the conductor. He is one of the great "sons of Korah" and is standing in front of all the singers, musicians, and dancers. You sense that today is a special day of worship and the goose bumps are already forming on your arm.
The conductor motions with his hand and the choir stands and begins to sing:

> *Hallelujah!*
> *Praise God in his holy place. Praise him in his great expanse. Praise him for his mighty works. Praise him according to his excellent greatness.* The choir sings the stanzas over and over again as they break into different melodies and harmonies. The men and the women sing antiphonally at times. One section of the choir would sing one line while another section sings a different line but in glorious harmony. The chills ran up and down your spine. Then the choir director announced, *Praise him with trumpet sounding.*

He motions toward the trumpet players and they begin to blow their instruments. There were all kinds of trumpets, big and small. The deep rumble of the large trumpets were in perfect harmony with the high sounds of the small trumpets. Their music blended into the singing of the choir and together the praise of God became louder and more glorious. The conductor now announced,

> *Praise him with stringed instrument and harp.*

The string section of the orchestra and the harpists began playing their instruments. They had every string instrument you had ever seen or heard. They blended their playing into the singing and trumpet music. He now announced,

Praise him with tambourine and dancing.

Immediately, the dancers ran to the front and began dancing as they shook and banged their tambourines and moved in perfect harmony with the singing and musicians. The conductor motioned to the string and wind sections and announced,

Praise him with stringed and wind instruments.

The music became louder as the new musicians accompanied the dancers. He then pointed to the brass section and announced,

Praise him with loud cymbals.
Praise him with reverberating cymbals.

They had all different sizes and kinds of cymbals, big and small. They played their instruments in harmony with the singing of the choir, the other musicians, and the dancers.

As you listened to and watched the singers, musicians, and dancers, you felt yourself transported into heaven itself and that you were at the very throne of YHWH with the heavenly choirs of angels and saints singing and making melody to the Lord.

Then the conductor turned to face the congregation and announced,

Let everyone who breathes praise YHWH.

He motioned to you and all the people assembled to join into the worship of God. The "Hallelujah" refrain and the stanzas had been repeated since the beginning and everyone knew how to sing it by now.

With tears streaming down your cheeks, you joined the entire assembly in singing and shouting *"Hallelujah!"* Some people ran forward and joined the dancers, whirling, singing, and shouting praises to the God of Israel.

After the choir, the musicians, the dancers, and the people were physically and emotionally exhausted in praise and worship, the conductor brought it all to a glorious climax with the trumpets and cymbals signaling it was time to stop.

You lived in the afterglow of that worship service for weeks and you will remember that day as long as you live.

Do not hesitate, like Handel, to see and hear the music found in the Bible. It is everywhere and echoes the music of heaven itself.

Musical Interludes

This is what the word "selah" is all about. It was left untranslated by the KJV translators because they did not know what the word originally meant.

Today, it is common knowledge that "selah" is a term that indicates where an instrumental interlude takes place. The singers pause at that place as the orchestra kept on playing. You can follow the inspired Torah to take a musical interlude by stopping and singing a favorite hymn, chorus or song. I found this practice helpful and experienced greater joy in reading a Psalm when I took a musical interlude.

BOOK I (Psalms 1-41)

The first Psalm in each of the Five Scrolls of the Psalms sets the theme and tone of the Psalms that follow. Psalm 1 tells us that believers do not live the same way that unbelievers live. There is a contrast between the righteous believers and the wicked unbelievers.

Is your life different from the unbelievers around you? If you hang out with unbelievers and do the same things they do, then you are not a true believer. Your life must match your lip. Your talk must match your walk. You must believe as you live and live as you believe.

The First Scroll collects those Psalms that emphasize that the wicked persecute the righteous by slander, gossip, and threats of murder. The righteous do not answer in kind but give their reputation to God for Him to vindicate them.

The first and second most condemned sins in the Psalms are slander and gossip. The wicked always persecute the righteous by attacking their character and motives. For an in-depth biblical study of gossip and slander see my book: *A Bible Handbook on Slander and Gossip.*

This is one way to distinguish the righteous from the wicked. Look to see who is using slander and gossip to persecute others. They are the wicked for whom the mists of darkness are reserved forever.

Psalm 1

The Way of the Righteous and the Wicked Contrasted

How blessed is the person:
  who does not walk according to the advice of the wicked,
  who does not stand on the path with sinners,
  who does not sit in the seat of mockers.
But-
  He delights in the Torah of YHWH,
  He meditates on his Torah day and night.
  He will be like a tree planted by streams of water,
    yielding its fruit in its season,
    whose leaf does not wither.
  He will prosper in everything he does.
But-
  This is not the case with the wicked:
    They are like chaff that the wind blows away.
    The wicked will not stand in the judgment,
    Nor sinners in the assembly of the righteous.
For-
    YHWH knows the way of the righteous,
But-
    the way of the wicked will be destroyed.

Psalm 2

The Futile Revolt of the Wicked Against God's Sovereignty

The Heathen Rage

Why are the heathen nations in an uproar?
Why are their people hatching a vain plot?
For-
    The kings of the earth take their stand;
    The rulers conspire together;
        against YHWH;
        against his Messiah.
  They say,
        "Let us tear off their shackles from us,
        Let us cast off their chains."

He who sits enthroned in the heavens laughs;
    the Sovereign Lord scoffs at them.
In his anger-
    he rebukes them,
In his wrath-
    he terrifies them *saying*:
        "Yea-
        I have set my King on Zion, my holy mountain."

Let me declare the decree of YHWH that he said to me:
    "You are my son,
      today I have become your father.
      Ask of me:
          I will give you the nations as your inheritance,
          I will give you even the ends of the earth as your possession.
      You will break them with an iron rod,
      You will shatter them like pottery."

"Therefore-
    O Kings-
        act wisely!
    O Earthly rulers-
        be warned!
Serve YHWH with fear,
Rejoice with trembling.
Kiss the Son before:
    he becomes angry,
      you will perish where you stand.
Indeed-
     his wrath can flare up quickly.
How blessed are those who take refuge in him."

Psalm 3

A song of David, when he fled from his son Absalom.

God Delivers the Righteous from the Wicked

O YHWH!
    How many are my persecutors!
    Many are rising up against me!
    Many are saying about me,
        "There is no deliverance for him in God!"

But you are,
O YHWH!
  A shield around me,
    My glory,
        The One who lifts up my head.

I cry to YHWH,
    he answers me from his holy mountain.

Musical Interlude

I lie down,
  I peacefully sleep,
    I wake up refreshed,
Because-
      YHWH sustains me.
I will not fear 10,000 enemies,
    who set themselves against me on every side.

Arise!
  O YHWH!
Deliver me!
  O my God!
For-
   you strike the jaw of all my enemies,
   you break the teeth of the wicked.
Deliverance comes from YHWH!
May your blessing be on your people.

Musical Climax

Psalm 4

To the Choir Director: With stringed instruments. A song of David

The Righteous Trust In God

When I call,
  answer me!
O my righteous God!
When I was in distress,
  you set me free.
Be gracious to me!
Hear my prayer!

You people,
    How long will you malign my reputation?
    How long will you love what is vain?
    How long will you love what is false?

Musical Interlude

  But-
  understand this:
    YHWH has set apart the godly for himself!
    YHWH will hear me when I cry out to him!
  Be angry-
  Yet-
    do not sin while doing so.
  Think about this when on your beds.
    Then be silent.

Musical Interlude

  Offer sacrifices of righteousness.
  Put your ultimate confidence in YHWH.

Many are asking,
   "Who will help us to see better days?"

O YHWH!
May the light of your face shine upon us.

You have given me more joy in my heart than at harvest times,
   when grain and wine abound.
I will both lie down and sleep in peace.

For-
you alone,
   O YHWH!
Enable me to rest securely.

Psalm 5

The Righteous Cry to God for Deliverance

To the Choir Director: For flutes. A song of David

    O YHWH!
      Listen to my words!
        Consider my groaning!
          Pay attention to my cry for help,
            my king and my God,
    for-
        unto you will I pray.

O YHWH!
In the morning-
      you will hear my voice;
In the morning-
        I will present my prayer to you,
        I will wait for your answer.

Indeed-
        You are not a God who delights in wickedness;
        Evil does not dwell with you.
        Boastful ones will not stand before you;
        You hate all those who practice wickedness.
        You will destroy those who speak lies.
YHWH abhors the person of bloodshed and deceit.

    But—
      I will come into your house,
        (because of the abundance of your gracious love)
    In awe of you-

I will worship in your holy Temple.

O YHWH!
  Lead me in your righteousness because of my enemies.
  Make your path straight before me.

But-
  as for the wicked,
    in their mouth there is no truthfulness,
    in them there is only wickedness.
Their throat is an open grave,
Their tongue is deceitful flattery.
Declare them guilty,
O God!
Let them fall by their own schemes.
Drive them away because of their many transgressions,
For-
    they have rebelled against you.

Let all those who take refuge in you rejoice!
Let them shout for joy forever.
May you protect them.
Let those who love your name exult in you.
Indeed-
  you will bless the righteous one.

O YHWH!
  Like a large shield,
    you will surround him with favor.

Psalm 6

The Righteous Cry to God in Times of Trouble

To the Choir Director: With stringed instruments. On an eight-stringed harp. A song of David

    O YHWH!
        in your anger- do not rebuke me,
        in your wrath- do not discipline me.

    O YHWH!
        Be gracious to me!
        Because-
            I am fading away.
        Heal me!
        Because-
            my body is distressed.
            my soul is deeply distressed.

    But you,
    O YHWH!
        How long do I have to wait for you?

    Return to me!
    O YHWH!
    Save my life!
    Deliver me!
        Because of your gracious love.
        Because in death, there is no public memorial of you.
        Because who will give you public thanks in the afterlife?

    I am weary from my groaning.
    Every night:
        My couch is drenched with tears,
        My bed is soaked through.

My eyesight has faded because of grief,
My eyesight has dimmed because of all my enemies.

Get away from me!
All of you who practice evil,
for-
    YHWH has heard the sound of my weeping.
    YHWH has heard my plea;
    YHWH receives my prayer.

As for all my enemies:
    They will be put to shame;
    They will become greatly frightened;
    They will suddenly be put to shame.

Psalm 7

A Psalm of David

Because of persecution from Cush the Benjamite, David cries to YHWH to vindicate him.

> O YHWH!
> My God!
> I seek refuge in you.
>
> Deliver me from those who persecute me!
> Rescue me!
> Lest like a lion-
> > they rip me to shreds,
> > > tearing me to pieces with no one to rescue me.
>
> O YHWH!
> My God!
> If-
> > I have done this thing,
> > I have done injustice with my hands,
> > I have rewarded those who did me good with evil,
> > I have plundered my enemy without justification,
>
> Then-
> > let my enemy pursue me,
> > let him overtake me,
> > let him trample my life to the ground.
> > let him put my honor into the dust.

Musical Interlude

> Rise up!
> O YHWH!
>
> In your anger,

Rise up!
Because-
   of the fury of my enemies.

 Arouse yourself for me!
 Command justice for me!

Let the assembly of the peoples gather around you,
For-
    You will sit high above them.
    YHWH will judge the peoples.

Judge me according to my righteous cause.
O YHWH!

 Judge me according to my integrity.
 O Exalted One!

 Let the evil of the wicked come to an end,
 But-
     establish the righteous.
 For-
     you are the righteous God who discerns the inner thoughts.

God is my shield,
God is the One who delivers the upright in heart.
God is a righteous judge.
God is angry with sinners every day.

 If-
    The ungodly one does not repent,
    God will sharpen his sword;
    God will string his bow and prepare it.
    He prepares weapons of death for himself.
    He makes his arrows into fiery shafts.

But-
> The wicked one travails with evil.
> He conceives malice.
> He gives birth to lies.
> He digs a pit,
>> even excavates it;
>>> then he falls into the hole that he had made.
> The troubles he planned for me,
>> will return on his own head.
> The violence he planned against me,
>> will come down on top of his head.

But-
as for me-
> I will praise YHWH for his righteousness,
> I will sing to the name of YHWH Most High.

Psalm 8

To the Choir Director: On a stringed instrument. A song of David

O YHWH!
Our sovereign Lord!
How excellent is your name in all the earth!
You have set your glory above the heavens!

Out of the mouths of infants and nursing babies;
You have established strength.

Because of your adversaries,
You silence the enemy and vengeful foe.

When I look at the heavens,
   the work of your fingers,
     the moon,
     the stars that you established—
what is man that you take notice of him?
     what is the son of man that you pay attention to him?

You made him a little less than God,
But-
   You crowned him with glory and honor.
   You gave him dominion over the work of your hands,
   You put all things under his feet:
     Sheep and cattle—all of them,
     wild creatures of the field,
       birds in the sky,
       fish in the sea—
     whatever moves through the currents of the oceans.
O YHWH!
Our sovereign Lord!
How excellent is your name in all the earth!

Psalm 9

To the Choir Director: Accompanied by female voices.

The Righteous Cry to God for Vindication

> I will give thanks to YHWH with all my heart,
> I will declare all your wonderful deeds.
> I will be glad and exult in you;
> I will sing praises to your name,
> O Most High!

When my enemies are turned back,
> They will stumble and perish before you.

For-
> You have brought about justice for me and my cause.
> You sit on the throne judging righteously.
> You rebuked the heathen nations,
> You destroyed the wicked,
> You wiped out their name forever and ever.

The enemy has perished,
The enemy is reduced to ruins forever.
You uprooted their cities,
> the very memory of them vanished.

But-

YHWH sits on his sovereign throne forever;
> His throne is established for judgment.

Thus-
> He will judge the world in righteousness
> He will make just decisions for the people.

YHWH is a refuge for the oppressed,
YHWH is a refuge in times of distress.

Those who know your name will place their ultimate
    confidence in you,
For-
    You have not forsaken those who seek you,
O YHWH!

Sing praises to YHWH who dwells in Zion.
Declare his mighty deeds among the peoples.
As an avenger of blood:
   he remembers them;
   he has not forgotten the cry of the afflicted.

Be gracious to me!
O YHWH!
Take note of my affliction,
Because-
    of those who hate me.
You snatch me away from the gates of death,
    so I may declare all your praise
        in the gates of the daughter of Zion,
    so I will rejoice in your deliverance.

The heathen nations have sunk down into the afterlife they
  made,
    their feet are ensnared in the snare they set for me.
YHWH has made himself known,
    executing judgment.
The wicked are ensnared,
    by what their hands have made.

Musical Interlude

   The wicked will turn back to the afterlife;
       With all the heathen nations that have forgotten God.

For-
> he will not always overlook the plight of the poor,
> he will not always overlook the hope of the afflicted forever.

Rise up!
O YHWH!
Do not let man prevail!

The heathen nations will be judged in your presence.
Make them afraid!
  O YHWH!
Let the heathen nations know that they are only men.

Musical Climax

Psalm 10

God Will Deliver Us and Judge the Wicked

Why do you stand far away from me?
  O YHWH!
Why do you hide from me in times of distress?

In arrogance the wicked one pursues the afflicted,
    who are trapped in the schemes he devises.
For-
      the wicked boasts about his own desire.
      the wicked blesses the greedy.
      the wicked despises YHWH.
 In his haughty arrogance the wicked thinks,
    "God will not execute justice."
  All his plans assume-
    "There is no God."

His ways seem always prosperous.
Your judgments seem to be on high far away from him.
    Thus he scoffs at all his enemies.
He says to himself,
        "I will not be moved from one generation to the next.
         I will not experience adversity."

His mouth is full of curses, lies, and oppression,
His tongue spreads trouble and iniquity.
He waits in ambush in the villages.
He kills the innocent in secret.
His eyes secretly watch the helpless,
He secretly lies like a lion in wait in his den,
He lies in wait to catch the afflicted.
He catches the afflicted when he pulls him into his net.
His victim is crushed and sinks down;
The helpless falls by his strength.

The wicked says to himself,
    "God has forgotten,
    God has hidden his face,
    God will never see it."
Rise up!
  O YHWH!
Raise your hand!
  O God!
Do not forget the afflicted!

Why does the wicked despise God?
Why does the wicked say to himself,
    "God will not seek justice."
But-
  You do see!
  You do take note of trouble and grief to take it into your hand.

The helpless one commits himself to you;
Because-
  You have been the helper of the orphan.

Break the arm of the wicked and evil man.
Seek out his wickedness until you find none.

YHWH is Sovereign King forever and ever!
Heathen nations have perished from his land.

O YHWH!
  You heard the desire of the afflicted;
  You will establish their heart,
  You will incline your ear,
    to do justice for the orphan and the oppressed,
    so that the wicked may cause terror no more.

Psalm 11

To the Choir Director: A song of David

Put Your Trust in God

>I take refuge in YHWH.
>So-
>>how can you say to me,
>>>"Flee like a bird to the mountains!"
>
>Look!
>The wicked have:
>>bent their bow,
>>placed their arrow on the string:
>>>to shoot from the darkness at the upright in heart.
>
>When the foundations are destroyed,
>>what can the righteous do?
>
>YHWH is in his holy Temple.
>YHWH's sovereign throne is in the heavens.
>His eyes behold,
>He examines the children of men.
>
>YHWH examines the righteous,
> But-
>>the wicked and those who love violence,
>
>He hates.
>He rains on the wicked burning coals and sulfur;
>>a scorching wind is their destiny.
>
>Indeed-
>>YHWH is righteous;
>>>he loves righteousness;
>>>>the upright will behold his face.

Psalm 12

To the Choir Director: On an eight stringed harp. A song of David

The Wicked are Greater in Number than the Righteous

   Help!
    O YHWH!
   For-
      Godly people have ceased to exist.
      Honest people have disappeared from among the children of men.
      Everyone speaks lies to his neighbor.
      They speak with slippery lips and hidden motives.
         (YHWH will cut off all slippery lips)
      Their tongue boasts great things,
       those who say:
         "By our tongues we will prevail;
         our lips belong to us.
         Who is lord over us?"
   Says YHWH,
      "Because of the oppression of the poor,
      Because of the sighing of the needy,
      I will now arise."
   Says YHWH,
      "I will set in safety those who yearn for it."

The words of YHWH are pure words,
    Like fine silver refined in an earthen furnace,
    purified seven times over.
O YHWH!
You will keep them safe.
   You will guard them forever from this generation.

In contrast-
The wicked:
   keep walking around,
      exalting the vileness of the children of men.

Psalm 13

To the Choir Director: A song of David

A Prayer for Deliverance

    How long?
O YHWH!
    Will you forget me forever?

    How long?
    Will you hide your face from me?

    How long must I struggle in my soul at night?
    How long must I have sorrow in my heart during the day?
    How long shall my enemy rise up against me?

    Look at me!
    Answer me!
    O YHWH!
    My God!

    Give light to my eyes:
        lest I sleep in death,
        lest my enemy say, "I have overcome him;"
        lest my persecutor rejoice when I am shaken.

    But-
    as for me-
        I have put my ultimate confidence in your gracious love,
        My heart will rejoice in your deliverance.
        I will sing to YHWH,
        For-
            he has dealt bountifully with me.

Psalm 14

To the Choir Director: A song of David

The Wicked are Fools

>Fools say within themselves,
>>"There is no God."
>
>They are corrupt and commit evil deeds;
>>not one of them practices what is good.
>
>YHWH looks down from the heavens upon humanity to see if anyone really searches for God.
>But-
>>All have turned away,
>>Together they have become corrupt;
>>No one practices what is good,
>>>not even one.
>
>Will those who do evil ever learn?
>They devour my people like they devour bread.
>They never call on YHWH.
>There they are seized with terror,
>Because-
>>God is with the generation of the righteous.
>
>You will frustrate the plans of the oppressors,
>Because-
>>YHWH is their refuge.
>
>Would that Israel's deliverance come out of Zion!
>When YHWH restores the fortunes of his people,
>>Jacob will rejoice,
>>Israel will be glad.

Psalm 15

To the Choir Director: A song of David

How to Enter God's Presence

   O YHWH!
   Who may dwell in your tabernacle?
   Who may dwell on your holy mountain?
     The one-
       who lives with integrity,
       who does righteous deeds,
       who speaks truth in his heart,
       who does not slander with his tongue,
       who does no evil to his neighbor,
       who does not destroy his friend's reputation,
       who despises those who are utterly wicked,
       who honors the one who fears YHWH,
       who keeps his word even when it hurts,
       who does not change his word,
       who does not loan his money for interest,
       who does not take a bribe against the innocent.

   The one who does these things will stand firm forever.

Psalm 16

A special Psalm of David

The righteous trust in God even in the Face of Death

   Keep me safe!
   O God!
   For-
   I take refuge in you!

   I said to YHWH,
      "You are my sovereign Lord,
       I have nothing good apart from you."

   As for the saints that are in the land,
      they are noble,
      all my delight is in them.

   Those who hurry after another god will multiply sorrows;
   I will not present their drink offerings of blood,
      nor will my lips speak their names.

   YHWH is my inheritance,
   YHWH is my cup of blessing;
      you will support my case.
   The boundary lines have fallen in pleasant places for me;
   Truly-
      I have a beautiful heritage.

   I will bless YHWH who has counseled me;
   Indeed-
      my thoughts have corrected me during the night.

   I will set YHWH before me continually;
   Because-

    he is at my right hand.

I will stand firm.
Therefore-
    my heart is glad,
    my glory rejoices,
    my body will dwell securely.
For-
    You will not abandon my soul in the afterlife,
    You will not allow your holy one to experience corruption,
    You will cause me to know the path of life.

In your presence is fullness of joy,
At your right hand there are pleasures forever.

Psalm 17

A prayer of David

A Cry for Justice

>O YHWH!
>Hear my just plea!
>>Pay attention to my cry!
>Give ear to my prayer,
>>since it does not come from lying lips.
>Justice for me will come from your presence;
>>your eyes see what is right.
>
>When-
>>You probe my heart,
>>>You will examine me at night;
>>
>When-
>>You refine me,
>>>You will find nothing,
>>
>For-
>>I have determined that I will not transgress with my mouth.
>
>As for the ways of mankind,
>I have-
>>according to the words of your lips,
>>avoided the ways of the violent.
>
>My steps have held fast to your paths,
>>thus my footsteps have not faltered.
>I call upon you,
>For-
>>you will answer me.

O God!
Turn your ear toward me!
Hear my prayer!
Show forth your gracious love!

Save those who take refuge in you from those who rebel against your sovereign power.

Protect me as the most precious part of the eye;
Hide me under the shadow of your wings from:
    the wicked who have afflicted me,
        my enemies who have surrounded me.

They are imprisoned by their own prosperity,
They have boasted in pride with their mouth.
    (Now they have enriched our paths)
They set their eyes to cast us down to the ground.
Like a lion they desire to rip us to pieces,
    like a young lion waiting in ambush.

Arise!
O YHWH!
Confront them to their face!
Bring them to their knees!
By your sword deliver me from the wicked,
   From mere men.

O YHWH!
By your hand deliver me from mere men of the world,
   whose reward is only in this life.

But-
   as for your treasured ones:
      may their stomachs be full,
      may their children have an abundance,
      may they leave wealth to their offspring.

But-
as for me,
   in righteousness I will behold your face;

When I awake,
   your presence will fully satisfy me.

Psalm 18

To the Choir Director: By the servant of YHWH, David, who spoke the words of this song to YHWH on the day when YHWH delivered him from the hands of all his enemies and from the hand of Saul.

The King Gives Thanks for Victory

>He said,
>>"I love you!
>>>O YHWH!
>>>My strength!"

>YHWH is-
>>my rock,
>>my fortress,
>>my deliverer,
>>my God,
>>my stronghold in whom I take refuge,
>>my shield,
>>the glory of my salvation,
>>my high tower.

>I cried out to YHWH,
>>who is worthy to be praised,
>I was delivered from my enemies.

>The cords of death entangled me;
>The rivers of Belial made me afraid.
>The cords of the afterlife surrounded me;
>The snares of death confronted me.

>In my distress I cried to YHWH;
>To my God I cried for help.

From his temple he heard my voice,
my cry reached his ears.

The world shook and trembled;
The foundations of the mountains quaked,
They shook because he was angry.
In his anger:
> smoke poured out of his nostrils,
> consuming fire from his mouth;
> coals were lit from it.

He bowed the heavens and descended,
> darkness was under his feet.

He rode upon a cherub and flew;
He soared upon the wings of the wind.
He made darkness his hiding place,
His canopy surrounding him was dark waters and thick clouds.
The brightness before him scattered the thick clouds,
> with hail stones and flashes of fire.

Then-
> YHWH thundered in the heavens,
> The Most High uttered his voice with hail stones and flashes of fire.
> He shot his arrows and scattered them;
> He frightened them with many lightning bolts.

Then-
> the channels of the sea could be seen,
> the foundations of the earth were uncovered,
> because of your rebuke.

O YHWH!
Because-
> of the blast from the breath of your nostrils.

He sent from on high and took me;
He drew me from many waters.
He delivered me from my strong enemies,
    even from those who hate me
    because-
        they were stronger than I.
They overcame me in the day of my calamity,
But-
    YHWH was my support.
He brought me out to a spacious place;
He delivered me,
For-
    in me he takes delight.

YHWH will reward me
because-
    of my righteous cause,
    of the cleanness of my hands-
        he will restore me;
    I have kept the ways of YHWH,
    I have not wickedly departed from my God;
    all his judgments were always before me,
    I did not cast off his statutes.
    I was upright before him,
    I kept myself from my iniquity.

So YHWH restored me according to my integrity,
Because-
    my hands were clean in his sight.

With the holy-
    you show your gracious love,
With the upright-
    you show yourself upright;

With the pure-
    you show yourself pure,
With the devious-
    you show yourself astute.

Indeed-
you deliver the oppressed,
But-
    you bring down those who exalt themselves in their own eyes.
For-
You,
  O YHWH!
Make my lamp shine!

My God brightens my darkness.
   By you I will run through an army,
   By my God I leap over a wall.

As for God,
   his way is upright;
   the word of God is pure;
   he is a shield to all those who take refuge in him.

For-
Who is God but YHWH?
Who is a Rock other than our God?—
  the God who clothes me with strength:
   who makes my way upright;
   who makes my feet swift as the deer;
   who makes me stand on the height;
   who teaches my hands to make war,
   who teaches my arms to bend a bronze bow.

You have given to me the shield of your deliverance,
   your right hand holds me up;

your gentleness made me great.
You make a broad place for my steps,
    so my feet would not slip.
I pursued my enemies;
I overtook them;
I did not turn around until they were utterly defeated.
I struck them down,
    so they are not able to rise up;
        they fell under my feet.
You clothed me with strength for war;
You will subdue under me those who rise up against me.
You have made my enemies turn their back to me,
    I will destroy those who hate me.
They cried out for deliverance,
But-
    there was no one to deliver;
They cried out to YHWH,
But-
    he did not answer them.

I ground them as dust before the wind;
I emptied them out like dirt in the street.

You rescued me from conflict with the people;
You made me head of the nations.
People who did not know me will serve me.
When they hear of me,
    they will obey me;

Foreigners will submit to me.
Foreigners will wilt away;
They will come trembling out of their stronghold.

YHWH lives!
Blessed be my Rock!
May the God of my deliverance be exalted!

He is the God who executes vengeance on my behalf;
    who destroys peoples under me;
    who delivers me from my enemies.

Truly-
    you will exalt me above those who rise up against me;
    you will deliver me from the violent person.
Therefore-
    I will give thanks to you among the heathen nations.

O YHWH!
    I will sing praises to your name.

He is the One:
    who gives victories to his king;
    who shows gracious love to his anointed,
    who shows gracious love to David,
    and his seed forever.

Psalm 19

To the Choir Director: A song of David

The heavens are declaring the glory of God,
   Their expanse shows the work of his hands.

Day after day they pour forth speech,
   Night after night they reveal knowledge.

There is no speech nor are there words where their voice is not heard.
Their message goes out into all the world,
Their words to the ends of the earth.

In the heavens he has set up a tent for the sun:
   it is like a bridegroom coming out of his chamber,
   it is like a champion who rejoices at the beginning of a race.
its circuit is from one end of the sky to the other,
   Nothing is hidden from its heat.

The Torah of YHWH is perfect,
   restoring life.
The testimony of YHWH is steadfast,
   making foolish people wise.
The precepts of YHWH are upright,
   making the heart rejoice.
The commandment of YHWH is pure,
   giving light to the eyes.
The fear of YHWH is clean,
   standing forever.
The judgments of YHWH are true;
   they are altogether righteous.
They are more desirable than gold,
   even much fine gold.

They are sweeter than honey,
    even the drippings from a honeycomb.
Moreover your servant is warned by them;
    and there is great reward in keeping them.

Who can detect his own mistakes?
Cleanse me from hidden sin.

Preserve your servant from arrogant people;
Do not let them rule over me.
Then-
    I will be upright,
    I will be acquitted of great wickedness.

May the words of my mouth,
May the meditations of my heart,
    be acceptable in your sight,
        O YHWH!
My Rock!
My Redeemer!

Psalm 20

To the Choir Director: A song of David

    May YHWH answer you in the day of distress;
    May the name of the God of Jacob lift you up on high.
    May he send you help from the sanctuary;
    May he sustain you from Zion.
    May he remember all your gifts;
    May he accept your burnt offerings.

Musical Interlude

    May he give you what is in your heart;
    May he fulfill all your plans.
    May we shout for joy at your deliverance
    May we unfurl our banners in the name of our God.
    May YHWH fulfill all your petitions.

    Now I know that:
        YHWH has delivered his anointed;
        he has answered him from his sanctuary,
        with the strength of his right hand of deliverance.

    Some-
        boast in chariots,
        others boast in horses;
    But-
        we will boast in the name of YHWH our God.

    While they bowed down and fell,
    We arose and stood upright.

Deliver us!
  O YHWH!
Answer us!
  O King-
    on the day we cry out!

Psalm 21

To the Choir Director: A song of David

The king rejoices in your strength,
O YHWH!

How greatly he rejoices in your deliverance.
You have granted him the desire of his heart,
You have not withheld the request of his lips.

Musical Interlude

You go before him with wonderful blessings,
You put a crown of fine gold on his head.

He asked life from you,
You gave it to him—
    length of days for ever and ever.
Great is his glory through your deliverance,
    honor and majesty you have placed upon him.
Indeed-
    you have given him eternal blessings;
    you will make him glad with the joy of your presence.

The king trusts in YHWH;
Because-
of the gracious love of the Most High,
    he will stand firm.

Your hand will find all your enemies,
Your right hand will find those who hate you.
When you appear,
O YHWH,
you will make them like a furnace of fire.

In his wrath he will consume them,
The fire will devour them.
You will destroy their descendants from the earth,
    even their offspring from the children of mankind.
Though they plot evil against you and devise schemes,
    they will not succeed.
Indeed-
you will make them retreat,
    when your bow is strung against their faces.

Rise up!
    O YHWH!
In your strength!
    And we will sing and praise your power.

Psalm 22

*To the Choir Director: To the tune of "Doe of the Dawn".
A song of David*

The Suffering Messiah

> My God!
> My God!
>
> Why have you abandoned me?
> Why are you so far from delivering me?
> Why are you so far from my groaning?
>
> O my God!
> I cry out to you throughout the day,
> But-
> > you do not answer;
>
> I call out to you throughout the night,
> But-
> > I have no rest.
>
> You are holy-
> > enthroned on the praises of Israel.
>
> Our ancestors trusted in you:
> > They trusted and you delivered them.
> > They cried out to you and escaped;
> > They trusted in you and were not put to shame.
>
> But-
> as for me-
> > I am only a worm and not a man,
> > I am scorned by mankind and despised by people.

Everyone who sees me mocks me:
    They gape at me with open mouths;
    They shake their heads at me.
      They say,
        "Commit yourself to YHWH;
          perhaps YHWH will deliver him,
          perhaps he will cause him to escape,
          since he delights in him."
Yet-
    you are the one who took me from the womb,
    you kept me safe on my mother's breasts.

I was dependent on you from birth;
From my mother's womb you have been my God.
Do not be so distant from me,
For-
      trouble is at hand;
      indeed-
      there is no other deliverer.

Many bulls have surrounded me;
The vicious bulls of Bashan have encircled me.
Their mouths are opened wide toward me,
    like roaring and attacking lions.

I am poured out like water;
All my bones are out of joint.
My heart is like wax,
    (It has melted within me),
My strength is dried up like broken pottery;
My tongue sticks to the roof of my mouth.

You have brought me down to the dust of death.
  For-
      Dogs have surrounded me;
      A gang of evil-doers have encircled me.

They pierced my hands and my feet.
I can count all my bones.

They look at me;
They stare at me.
They divide my clothing among themselves;
They cast lots for my clothing!

But-
as for you-
  O YHWH!
Do not be far away from me.

O my Strength!
Come quickly to help me!

Deliver me from the sword.
Deliver my precious soul from the power of the dog.
Deliver me from the mouth of the lion,
Deliver me from the horns of the wild oxen.

You have answered me.
Thus-
  I will declare your name to my brothers;
  I will praise you in the midst of the congregation, saying,
    "All who fear YHWH, praise him!
    All the seed of Jacob, glorify him!
    All the seed of Israel, fear him!
    For-
      he does not despise nor detest the afflicted
      because of his affliction;
      he does not hide his face from him,
      he hears him when he cries out to him."

My praise in the great congregation is because of you;
I will pay my vows before those who fear him.
The afflicted shall eat and be satisfied;
Those who seek YHWH shall praise him,
    "May you live forever!"

All the ends of the earth will remember and turn to YHWH;
All the families of the nations will bow in submission to YHWH.
Indeed-
    the kingdom belongs to YHWH;
    his sovereignty rules over the heathen nations.

All the prosperous people will eat and bow down in submission.
All those who are about to go down to the dust will bow down in submission,
Along with the one who can no longer keep himself alive.

Our descendants will serve him,
That generation will be told about the sovereign Lord.
They will come and declare his righteousness to a people yet to be born;
Indeed-
He has accomplished it!

Psalm 23

A song of David

Messiah Shepherds His People

> YHWH is continuously shepherding me all the time.
> Therefore-
> > I will never be in a situation where I lack anything.
>
> He makes me to lie down in pastures of green grass;
> He guides me beside quiet waters.
> He revives my soul;
> He leads me in the paths of righteousness for the sake of his name.
>
> Even when I walk through a ravine filled with dark shadows,
> > I will not be afraid,
>
> Because-
> > you are with me.
>
> Your rod and your staff—
> > they comfort me.
>
> You prepare a table before me,
> > even in the presence of my enemies;
>
> You anoint my head with oil;
> > my cup overflows.
>
> Truly-
> > Goodness and love will pursue me all the days of my life,
> > I will dwell in the house of YHWH forever.

Psalm 24

A song of David

King Messiah

> The earth and everything in it belongs to YHWH—
>> the world,
>> and all who live in it.
> Indeed-
>> he founded it upon the seas,
>> he established it upon deep waters.
>
> Who may ascend the mountain of YHWH?
> Who may stand in his Holy Place?
> The one-
>> who has innocent hands and a pure heart;
>> who does not delight in what is false
>> who does not swear an oath deceitfully.
> This person will receive blessing from YHWH,
>> This person will receive righteousness from the God of his salvation.
>
> This is the generation that seeks him:
>> Those who seek your face are the true seed of Jacob.

Musical Interlude

> Lift up your heads,
> O gates!
>
> Be lifted up,
> O ancient doors!
>
> The King of Glory is marching in.
> Who is he, this King of Glory?

YHWH strong and mighty;
YHWH mighty in battle.

Lift up your heads,
O gates!
Be lifted up,
O ancient doors!

The King of Glory is marching in.
Who is he, this King of Glory?
    YHWH of the Heavenly Armies—
    He is the King of Glory.

Musical Climax

Psalm 25

A song of David

His Prayer for Help and Forgiveness

   I will lift up my soul to you,
     O YHWH!

   I trust in you!
     O my God!

   Do not let shame come upon me;
   Do not let my enemies triumph over me.

   Indeed-
     no one who waits on you will be put to shame.
   But-
     those who offend for no reason will be put to shame.

   Cause me to understand your ways!
     O YHWH!
   Teach me your paths!

   Guide me in your truth and teach me;
   For-
     you are the God who delivers me.

   All day long I have waited for you.
   Remember me!
   O YHWH!
   Your tender mercies,
   Your gracious love;
   Indeed-
     they are eternal!

Do not remember my youthful sins and transgressions;
But-
Remember me:
    in the light of your gracious love,
    in the light of your goodness.
O YHWH!

YHWH is good and just;
Therefore-
    He will teach sinners concerning the way.
    He will guide the humble concerning justice;
    He will teach the humble his way.

All the paths of YHWH are gracious love and truth for those:
    who keep his covenant,
    who keep his decrees.

For the sake of your name,
O YHWH!
Forgive my sin!
For-
    it is great.

Who is the man who fears YHWH?
    God will teach him the path he should choose.
    He will experience good things;
    His descendants will inherit the earth.

The counsel of YHWH is for those who fear him in order that:
    they may know his covenant.
My eyes look to YHWH continually,
Because-
    he is the one who releases my feet from the trap.

Turn toward me!
Have mercy on me!

For-
> I am lonely and oppressed.
> The troubles on my heart have increased.

Bring me out of my distress!
Look upon my distress and affliction!
Forgive all my sins!

Look at how my enemies have multiplied;
> they hate me with a vicious hatred.
Preserve my life and deliver me;
> do not let me be put to shame,
>> because-
>>> I take refuge in you.
Integrity and justice will preserve me,
Because-
> I wait on you.

Redeem Israel!
O God!
From all her troubles.

Psalm 26

A song of David

A Man of Integrity Pleads for Vindication

   Vindicate me!
   O YHWH!
   Because-
      I have walked in integrity;
      I have trusted in YHWH without wavering.

   Examine me!
   O YHWH!
      Prove me!
      Test my heart and mind.
   For-
      your gracious love is before me,
      I continually walk according to your truth.
      I do not sit with those committed to what is false,
      I do not travel with hypocrites.
      I hate the company of evildoers,
      I do not sit with the wicked.
      I wash my hands in innocence.
      I go around your altar.

   O YHWH!
      I will praise you loudly with thanksgiving,
      I will declare all your wondrous acts.
   O YHWH!
      I love the dwelling place of your house,
         the place where your glory resides.

   Do not group me with sinners,
   Do not include me with men of bloodshed.

Their hands are filled with wicked schemes,
　　　Their right hands with bribes.

But-
　as for me,
　　　I walk in my integrity.
Redeem me!
Be gracious to me!

My feet stand on level ground.
In the midst of the worshipping congregations
　　　I will publicly bless YHWH.

Psalm 27

A song of David

Confidence in YHWH

> YHWH is my light and my salvation—
> > whom will I fear?
> YHWH is the strength of my life-
> > of whom will I be afraid?
>
> When evildoers, my enemies, and my oppressors come to devour my flesh-
> > they stumble and fall.
> If an army encamps against me-
> > my heart will not fear.
> If a war is launched against me-
> > I will even trust in that situation.
>
> I have asked one thing from YHWH.
> It is what I really seek:
> > That-
> > > I may dwell in the house of YHWH all the days of my life;
> > > I may gaze on the beauty of YHWH;
> > > I may inquire in his temple.
> > For-
> > > he will conceal me in his shelter on the day of evil;
> > > he will hide me in a secluded chamber within his tent;
> > > he will place me on a high rock.
> Now my head will be lifted up above my enemies,
> > even those who surround me.
>
> I will sacrifice in his tent with shouts of joy;
> I will sing and make melodies to YHWH.

Hear my voice!
O YHWH!
When I cry out:
    Be gracious to me.
    Answer me.

Concerning you,
    my heart recalls your word,
        "Seek my face."
So your face,
O YHWH,
I will seek.

Do not hide your face from me;
Do not turn away in anger from your servant.

You have been my help!
Therefore-
    do not abandon or forsake me!
O God of my salvation!

Though my father and my mother abandoned me,
YHWH will gather me up.

Teach me your way,
O YHWH!

Lead me on a level path because of my enemies.
Do not hand me over to the desires of my enemies;
For-
    false witnesses have risen up against me;
    even the one who breathes out violence.

I believe that I will see YHWH's goodness in the land of the living.

Wait on YHWH!
Be courageous!
He will strengthen your heart.
Wait on YHWH!

Psalm 28

A song Of David

A Prayer for Help

To you,
   O YHWH!
I cry out!

My Rock!
   Do not refuse to answer me.

If you refuse to answer me,
   I will become like those who descend into the afterlife.

Hear the sound of my supplications when I cry to you for help,
   as I lift up my hands toward your most holy sanctuary.

Do not drag me away with the wicked,
Do not drag me away with those who practice iniquity,
   who speak false peace to their neighbors,
   who harbor evil in their hearts.

Reward them according to their deeds-
   According to the evil of their actions.
Reward them according to work of their hands-
   According to what they deserve.
Because:
   They do not understand the deeds of YHWH,
   They do not understand the work of his hands.
He will tear them down,
He will never build them up.

Blessed be YHWH!
For-
   he has heard the sound of my supplications.

YHWH is my strength and my shield;
My heart trusts in him,
Because-
   I have received help.
My heart exalts;
   I give thanks to him with my song.

YHWH is the strength of his people;
   He is a refuge of deliverances for his anointed.

Deliver your people!
Bless your inheritance!
Shepherd them!
Lift them up forever!

Psalm 29

A song of David

Praise to the Sovereign YHWH

    Ascribe to YHWH,
      you heavenly beings.

    Ascribe to YHWH glory and strength.
    Ascribe to YHWH the glory due his name;
    Worship YHWH in holy attire.

    The voice of YHWH was heard above the waters;
    The voice of God of glory thundered;
    The voice of YHWH was heard over many waters.
    The voice of YHWH is powerful;
    The voice of YHWH is majestic.
    The voice of YHWH breaks the cedars.
    The voice of YHWH breaks the cedars of Lebanon-
        He makes them stagger like a calf-
            even Lebanon and Serion-
        like a young wild ox.
    The voice of YHWH shoots out flashes of fire.
    The voice of YHWH shakes the wilderness;
    The voice of YHWH shakes the wilderness of Kadesh.
    The voice of YHWH causes deer to give birth,
    The voice of YHWH strips the forest bare.
        In his temple all of them shout, "Glory!"

    YHWH sat enthroned over the flood.
    YHWH sits as sovereign king forever.
    YHWH will give strength to his people;
    YHWH will bless his people with peace.

Psalm 30

A song of David for the dedication of the temple

Thanksgiving for Deliverance

    I exalt you,
      O YHWH!
    For-
        you have lifted me up,
    Thus-
        my enemies could not gloat over me.

      O YHWH!
    My God!

    I cried out to you for help,
    You healed me.

      O YHWH!
    You brought me from death;
    You kept me alive so that I did not descend into the afterlife.

    You,
    his godly ones,
    Sing to YHWH!
    Give thanks at the mention of his holiness-
    For-
        his wrath is only momentary;
        his favor is for a lifetime.
    Weeping may endure for the night,
    But-
        shouts of joy will come in the morning.
    But,
    as for me-
    I said in my prosperity,

"I shall never be moved."

By your favor,
  O YHWH!
You established me as a strong mountain;
Then you hid your face,
I was dismayed.

I cried out to you,

  "O YHWH!"

I make supplication to YHWH:
    "What profit is there in my death if I go down to the afterlife?
    Can the dust publicly worship you?
    Can it publicly proclaim your faithfulness?"

 Hear me,
  O YHWH!

Have mercy on me!
  O YHWH!

Help me!

You have turned my mourning into dancing;
You took off my sackcloth,
You put on me a garment of joy,
so that:
    I may sing praise to you
    I may not remain silent.

  O YHWH!
 My God!

I will give you thanks forever!

Psalm 31

To the Choir Director: A song of David

Prayer and Thanksgiving

    In you alone,
    O YHWH!
    I have taken refuge.
    Let me never be put to shame.

    In your righteousness deliver me!
    Turn you ear toward me!
    Deliver me quickly!

    Become a rock of safety for me,
    Become a fortified citadel to deliver me.
    For-
        you are my rock and my fortress;
    For-
       the sake of your name:
          guide me;
          lead me.
    Get me out of the snare that they hid for me;
    For-
        you are my strength.

    Into your hands I commit my spirit;
    For-
        you have redeemed me.

    O YHWH!
    O God of truth!

    I despise those who trust vain idols;
    But-

I have trusted in YHWH.
I will rejoice and be glad in your gracious love,
For-
    you see my affliction
Take note of the distresses of my soul.
You have not delivered me into the hand of the enemy,
You have set my feet in a broad place.

Be gracious to me!
  O YHWH!
For I am in distress.

My eyes have been consumed by my grief
    along with my soul and my body.
My life is consumed by sorrow,
    my years with groaning.
My strength has faltered because of my iniquity;
    my bones have been consumed.

I have become an object of reproach to all my enemies,
    especially to my neighbors.
I have become an object of fear to my friends,
    whoever sees me outside runs away from me.
Like a dead man,
    I am no longer remembered in their minds—
        like broken pottery.

I have heard the slander of many;
It is like terror all around me,
As-
    they conspire together and plot to take my life.
But-
    I put my ultimate confidence in you,
      O YHWH!

I say,
   "You are my God.
   My times are in your hands.
   Deliver me from the hands of my enemies
   Deliver me from those who pursue me.
   May your face shine on your servant;
   in your gracious love, deliver me.
   Let me not be put to shame."

O YHWH!
I have called upon you alone!

Let the wicked be put to shame,
Let them be silent in the afterlife.
Let the lying lips be made still.
Even-
   those who speak arrogantly against the righteous-
   in pride and contempt.

How great is your goodness that you have stored up for:
   those who fear you,
   those who take refuge in you,
      in the presence of the children of men.

You will hide them in the secret place of your presence,
   away from the conspiracies of men.
You will hide them in your tent,
   away from their contentious tongues.

Blessed be YHWH!
In a marvelous way he demonstrated his gracious love to me,
   When I was in a fortified city.
      Where I said in my panic,
      "I have been cut off in your sight,"
Then-
   you surely heard the voice of my supplication in my plea

to you for help.

Love YHWH!
All his godly ones!

YHWH preserves the faithful;
YHWH repays those who act in pride.

Be strong!
Let your heart be courageous!
All you who put your ultimate hope in YHWH.

Psalm 32

A song of David

The Blessings of Forgiveness

> How blessed is the person-
>> whose transgression is forgiven,
>> whose sin is covered.
>
> How blessed is the person-
>> against whom YHWH does not charge iniquity,
>> in whose spirit there is no deceit.
>
> When I kept silent about my sin,
>> my body wasted away
>>> by my groaning all day long.
>
> For-
>> your hand was heavy upon me day and night;
>> my strength was exhausted
>>> as in a summer drought.

Musical Interlude

> I acknowledged my sin to you;
> I did not hide my iniquity.
>
> I said,
>> "I will confess my transgressions to YHWH."
>> And you forgave the guilt of my sin!

Musical Interlude

> Therefore-
>> every godly person should pray to you at such a time.
> Surely- a flood of great waters will not reach him.

You are my hiding place!
You will deliver me from trouble.
You surround me with shouts of deliverance.

Musical Interlude

I will instruct you and teach you concerning the path you should walk;
I will direct you with my eye.

Do not be like a horse or mule,
    without understanding.
They are held in check by a bit and bridle in their mouths;
They will not remain in your presence.

The wicked have many sorrows,
But-
    gracious love surrounds those who trust in YHWH.

O righteous ones,
    be glad in YHWH and rejoice!
Shout for joy,
    all of you who are upright in heart!

Psalm 33

Praise to the Creator and Deliverer

>Rejoice in YHWH!
>O you righteous ones;
>Because-
>>the praise of the upright is beautiful.
>
>With the lyre,
>>give thanks to YHWH;
>
>With the ten stringed harp,
>>play music to him;
>
>With a new song,
>>sing to him;
>
>With shouts of joy,
>>play skillfully.
>
>For the word of YHWH is upright;
>>All his works are done in faithfulness.
>
>He loves righteousness and justice;
>>the world is filled with the gracious love of YHWH.
>
>By the word of YHWH the heavens were made;
>>All the heavenly bodies were made by the breath of his mouth.
>
>He gathered the waters of the ocean into a heap;
>He put the deeps into storehouses.
>
>Let all the world fear YHWH;
>Let all the inhabitants of the world stand in awe of him;
>Because-
>>he spoke-
>>>it came to be,
>>
>>he commanded-

it stood fast.

YHWH makes void the counsel of nations;
He frustrates the plans of peoples.
But-
    YHWH's sovereignty will stand firm forever,
    The plans in his mind will stand firm for all generations.

How blessed is the nation whose God is YHWH,
    the people he has chosen as his own inheritance.
When YHWH looks down from heaven,
    he beholds every human being.
From his dwelling place,
    he looks down on all the inhabitants of the earth.
He formed the hearts of them all;
    he understands all of their works.

A king is not saved by a large army;
A mighty soldier is not delivered by his great strength.

It is vain to trust in a horse for deliverance,
    even with its great strength,
        it cannot deliver.
Indeed-
    the eye of YHWH is on those who fear him,
    on those who put their ultimate confidence in his gracious love:
        to deliver them from death;
        to keep them alive in times of famine.

We wait on YHWH;
    he is our help and our shield.
Indeed-
    our heart will rejoice in him,
because-
    we have placed our ultimate confidence in his holy name.

O YHWH!
May your gracious love be upon us,
   even as we hope in you.

Psalm 34

Of David, when he pretended to be insane before Abimelech, who drove him away. So David left.

Learning about God's Deliverance

    I will bless YHWH at all times;
    His praise will be in my mouth continually.
    My soul will glorify YHWH;
       the humble will hear about it and rejoice.

    Magnify YHWH with me!
    Let us lift up his name together!

    I sought YHWH;
       he answered me;
       he delivered me from all of my fears.

    Look to him and be radiant;
    You will not be ashamed.

    This poor man cried out,
    YHWH heard;
    He delivered him from all of his distress.

    The angel of YHWH surrounds those who fear him;
    He delivers them.

    Taste and see that YHWH is good!
    How blessed is the person who puts his ultimate confidence in him!

    Fear YHWH!
      You his holy ones;
    For-

those who fear him lack nothing.

Young lions lack and go hungry,
But-
    those who seek YHWH will never lack any good thing.
"Come,
Children,
  listen to me!
I will teach you the fear of YHWH.

Who among you desires life?
Who wants long life in order to see good?
Then-
    Keep your tongue from doing evil;
    Keep your lips from spreading lies.
    Avoid evil;
    Do good.
    Seek peace and pursue it."

The eyes of YHWH look kindly on the righteous,
The ears of YHWH are open to their cries.
The face of YHWH is set against those who do evil,
    he will remove memory of them from the earth.

YHWH hears those who cry out,
YHWH delivers them from all their distress.
YHWH is close to the brokenhearted,
YHWH delivers those whose spirit has been crushed.

A righteous person will have many troubles,
But-
    YHWH will deliver him from them all.
    God protects all his bones;
    Not one of them will be broken.

Evil will kill the wicked;
Those who hate the righteous will be held guilty.
YHWH redeems the lives of his servants;
None of those who put their ultimate confidence in him will be held guilty.

Psalm 35

A song Of David

A Prayer for Deliverance from Slander, Gossip, and Death Threats

Argue my case!
O YHWH!
Against those who argue against me.

Fight against those who fight against me.
Take up the buckler and the shield,
Rise up to help me.
Take out the spear and the ax to confront the one who pursues me;
Say to me,
    "I am your deliverer!"

Let those who seek my life be put to shame and disgraced;
Let those who plot evil against me be driven back and confounded.
Make them like the chaff before the wind,
    as the messenger of YHWH pushes them aside.
May their path be dark and slippery,
    as the messenger of YHWH tracks them down.

Without justification they laid a snare for me;
    without justification they dug a pit to trap me.
Let destruction come upon them unawares,
    let the net that he hid catch him;
    let him fall into destruction.

My soul will rejoice in YHWH;
My soul will be glad in his deliverance.
All my bones will say,
    "O YHWH!

> Who is like you?
> Who delivers-
>> the weak from the one who is stronger than he?
>> the weak and the needy from the one who wants to rob him?"

False witnesses stepped forward;
They questioned me concerning things about which I knew nothing.
They paid me back evil for good;
 My soul mourns.
But-
>> when they were sick,
>> I wore sack cloth,
>> humbled myself with fasting,
>> prayed from my heart repeatedly for them.
>> I paced about as for my friend or my brother,
>> I fell down mourning as one weeps for one's mother.
But-
> when I stumbled,
> They rejoiced,
> They gathered together.
> They gathered together against me—
>> attackers whom I did not know.
>> They tore me apart and would not stop.

Malicious mockers—
> they gnashed their teeth against me.
O sovereign Lord!
How long will you just watch?
Rescue me-
> from their destruction,
> my soul from these young lions.
Then-
> I will give you thanks in front of the great congregation;
> I will praise you in the midst of the mighty throng.

Do not let my deceitful enemies gloat over me,
Do not let those who hate me without justification mock me with their eyes.
For-
> they do not speak peace;
> they devise clever lies against the peaceful people of the land.
> they open their mouth wide against me, claiming,
>> "O Yes! O Yes! We saw him do it with our own eyes!"

Do you not see all this?
  O YHWH!
Please do not remain silent!

  O YHWH!
Do not be far from me!
Wake up!
Arouse yourself to vindicate me!
Argue my case!

My God and my sovereign Lord.
Judge me according to your righteousness,

O YHWH my God!
Do not let them gloat over me.
Do not let them say in their hearts,
  "O Yes! We got what we wanted."
Do not let them say,
  "We have swallowed him up."
Instead-
Let those who gloat over the evil directed against me:
  be ashamed;
  be confounded together;
Let those who exalt themselves over me
  be clothed with shame and dishonor.

Let those who delight in my vindication
    shout for joy and rejoice!
Let them continually say,
    "O magnify YHWH who delights in giving peace to his servant."

My tongue will declare your righteousness and praise you all day long.

Psalm 36

To the Choir Director: By the servant of YHWH, David

An Oracle from YHWH

> An oracle that came to me about the transgressions of the wicked:
>
> "There is no fear of God before his eyes.
> He flatters himself too much to acknowledge his transgression and hate it.
> The words from his mouth are vain and deceptive.
> He has abandoned behaving wisely and doing good.
> He devises iniquity on his bed and is determined to follow a path that
> is not good.
> He does not resist evil."

Praise to YHWH

Your gracious love,
O YHWH!
   Reaches to the heavens;
Your truth,
   extends to the skies.
Your righteousness,
   is like the mountains of God;
Your justice,
   is like the great depths of the sea.

You deliver both people and animals.
O YHWH!

How precious is your gracious love,
O God!

The children of men take refuge in the shadow of your wings.
They are refreshed from the abundance of your house;
You cause them to drink from the river of your pleasures.
For-
    With you is a fountain of life,
    In your light we will see light.

Send forth your gracious love to those who know you,
Send forth your righteousness to those who are upright in heart.
Do not let the foot of the proud crush me;
Do not let the hand of the wicked destroy me.

Those who do evil have fallen;
They have been thrown down,
They cannot get up.

Psalm 37

A song Of David

Trust in God and Fear Not What Man can Do To You

Do not be angry
   because of those who do evil.
Do not be jealous
   because of those who commit iniquity.
Indeed,
   they soon will wither like grass,
      like green herbs they will fade away.

Instead-
Put your full confidence in YHWH,
Do good,
Dwell in the land,
Feed on faithfulness.

Delight yourself in YHWH,
   and he will give you the desires of your heart.
Commit your way to YHWH;
Trust him,
   and he will do it.
He will bring forth your righteousness as a light,
   and your just cause as the noonday sun.

Be silent before YHWH
Wait patiently for him.
Do not be angry because of the one whose way prospers
Do not be angry because of the one who implements evil schemes.

Calm your anger;
Abandon wrath.
Do not be angry—
    it only leads to evil.
Those who do evil will perish.
But-
    those who wait on YHWH will inherit the land.

Yet-
    a little while longer,
    the wicked will be no more.
You will search for his place,
But-
    he will not be there.

The humble-
    will inherit the land;
    will take in abundant peace.

The wicked plots against the righteous,
The wicked grinds his teeth at him.
But-
    YHWH laughs at him;
    he sees that his day is coming!
The wicked take out a sword;
The wicked bend the bow-
    to bring down the humble and the poor
    to slay those who are righteous in conduct.
But-
    their sword will pierce their own heart,
    their bows will be broken!

Better is the little that the righteous have,
than the abundance of many wicked people.

For-
> the arms of the wicked will be broken

But-
> YHWH upholds the righteous.

YHWH knows the day of the blameless,
Their inheritance will last forever.
They will not experience shame in times of trouble;
In times of famine, they will have plenty.

Indeed-
> The wicked will perish.
> The enemies of YHWH will be consumed like flowers in the fields.
> They will vanish like smoke.

The wicked borrow but never pay back;
But-
> the righteous are generous and give.

Those blessed by God will inherit the land,
But-
> those cursed by him will be cut off.

A man's steps are established by YHWH,
YHWH delights in his way.

Though he stumbles,
> he will not finally fall down flat,
> > for-
> > > YHWH will hold up his hand.

I once was young and now I am old,
But-
> I have not seen-
> > a righteous person forsaken,
> > > or his descendants begging for bread.

Every day he is generous, lending freely,
his descendants are blessed.

Depart from evil!
Do good!
Then you will dwell in the land forever.

Indeed-
   YHWH loves justice,
   he will not abandon his godly ones.
   They are kept safe forever,
But-
   the descendants of the wicked will be cut off.

The righteous will inherit the land;
They will dwell in it forever.
The mouth of the righteous one produces wisdom;
his tongue speaks justice.

The Torah of his God is in his heart;
his steps will not slip.

The wicked stalks the righteous,
   seeking to kill him.

But-
   YHWH-
      will not let him fall into his hands.
      will not be condemned when he is put on trial.

O wait on YHWH!
Keep faithful to his way;
he will exalt you to possess the land.

You will see the wicked cut off.

I once observed a wicked and oppressive person,
    flourishing like a green tree in native soil.
But-
    then he passed away;
    in fact,
        he simply was not there.
When I looked for him-
    he could not be found.

Observe the blameless!
Take note of the upright!
Indeed-
    the future of that man is peace.

Sinners will be destroyed together;
The future of the wicked will be cut off.
But-
    deliverance for the righteous one comes from YHWH;
    he is their strength in times of distress.
YHWH helps and delivers them;
    he will deliver them from the wicked,
    he will save them because they have sought refuge in him.

Psalm 38

A song of David

He Cries out for Forgiveness and Vindication

    O YHWH!
        Do not rebuke me in your anger;
        Do not correct me in your wrath,
    Because-
        your arrows have sunk deep into me,
        your hand has come down hard on me.

    My body is unhealthy due to your anger,
    My bones have no rest due to my sin.

    My iniquities loom over my head;
        like a cumbersome burden,
            they are too heavy for me.

    My wounds have putrefied and festered
    Because-
        of my foolishness.
    I am bent over and walk about greatly bowed down;
    All day long I go around mourning.
    My insides are burning
    My body is unhealthy.

    I am weak and utterly crushed;
    I cry out in distress because of my heart's anguish.

    O sovereign Lord!
    All my longings are before you,
    All my groaning is not hidden from you.
    My heart pounds,
    My strength fails me,

even the gleam in my eye is gone.

As for my friends and my neighbors,
   they stand aloof from my distress;
      even my close relatives stand at a distance.
Those who seek my life lay snares for me;
Those who seek to do me harm brag all day long about their wicked planning.
I am like the deaf,
   who cannot hear,
I am like the mute,
   who cannot open his mouth.
Indeed-
I have become like a man who hears nothing,
   in whose mouth there is no rebuke.

Because-
   I have placed my hope in you.
O YHWH!
You will answer.

O sovereign Lord!
My God!
I said,
   "Do not let them gloat over me,
      as they congratulate themselves when my foot slips."

Indeed-
I am being set up for a fall,
I am continually reminded of my pain.
I confess my iniquity.

My sin troubles me.
My enemies are alive and well;
Those who hate me without a reason are many.

They reward my good with evil,
> opposing me because I seek to do good.

Do not forsake me!
O YHWH!
My God!
Do not be so distant from me!

Come quickly!
Help me!
O Sovereign Lord!
My Deliverer!

Psalm 39

To the Choir Director: To Jeduthun. A song of David

A Cry for God to hear his prayer

    I told myself:
        "I will keep watch over my tongue to keep from sinning.
        I will muzzle my mouth when the wicked are around."

        I was as silent as a mute person;
        I said nothing,
            not even something good,
            my distress deepened.
        My heart within me became hot;
        As I thought about it,
            the fire burned within me.

  Then my tongue spoke out:
        "O YHWH!
            Let me know my end,
            Let me know the measure of my days,
                whatever it is!
            Then I will know how transient my life is.
            Look!
            You have made my lifespan fit in your hand;
            It is nothing compared to yours.
            Surely every person at their best is only a puff of wind."

Musical Interlude

    In fact-
        people walk around as shadows.
    Surely-
        they busy themselves for nothing,
            heaping up possessions;

        not knowing who will get them.
How long?
O sovereign Lord,
Will I wait in expectation?
For-
    in you I have placed my ultimate hope.

Deliver me from all my transgressions,
Do not let fools scorn me."

I remain silent;
I do not open my mouth,
For-
    you are the one who did it!

Make your scourges go away from me;
Since-
    I have been crushed by your heavy hand.
With rebukes-
    you chasten a man with the consequence of his iniquities;
    like a moth,
    you destroy what is attractive to him.
Indeed-
    every person is only a puff of wind.

Musical Interlude

Hear my prayer!
O YHWH!
Pay attention to my cry!

Do not ignore my tears,
because-
    I am an alien in your presence,
    I am a stranger just like my ancestors were.

Stop staring at me so I can smile again,
before I depart and am no more.

Psalm 40

To the Choir Director: A Psalm of David

Prayer for Help and Praise to God

   I waited in expectation for YHWH,
   He took notice of me;
   He heard my cry.
   He lifted me out of a pit of loud confusion,
      even out of the quicksand;
   He placed my feet on a rock
   He established my steps.
   He put a new song in my mouth,
      Even praise to our God!
   Many will watch and be in awe,
      they will place their trust in YHWH.

   How blessed is that person of strength
      who places his trust in YHWH,
      who has not turned to the proud,
      who has not turned aside to lies.

   O YHWH!
   My God!
   You have done great things:
      marvelous works and your thoughts toward us.
   There is no one who compares to you!

   I will try to recite them,
      even though there are too many to number.

   You take no delight in sacrifices and offerings,
   You have prepared my ears to listen,
   You require no burnt offerings or sacrifices for sin.
   Then I said,

"Here I am!
I have come!
In the scroll of the book it is written about me.
I delight to do your will, O my God.
Your Torah is part of my inner being."

In the great congregation I have publicly proclaimed the good news of righteousness.
Behold!
    I did not seal my lips!

O YHWH!
You know:
    I have not covered over your righteousness in my heart;
    I have proclaimed your faithfulness and deliverance.
    I have not concealed your gracious love and truthfulness from the great congregation.
O YHWH!
Do not withhold your mercies from me:
    For your gracious love and truthfulness will keep me safe continuously.
    For many innumerable evils have surrounded me;
    For my iniquities have overtaken me so that I cannot see.
    For they are more in number than the hair on my head,
    For my heart has forsaken me.

O YHWH!
Be pleased to deliver me;

O YHWH!
Hurry up and help me!
    Let those who seek to destroy my life be both put to shame and confounded;
    Let them be driven backwards and humiliated, particularly those who wish me evil.

Let shame be the reward for those who say to me, "Aha! Aha!"
Let all who seek you shout for joy and be glad in you.

May those who love your deliverance say,
   "YHWH be magnified continuously."
But-
   I am poor and needy.

May the sovereign Lord notice me.
You are my only help and deliverer!

O my God!
Do not tarry too long!

Psalm 41

To the Choir Director: A song of David

Trust God When Things Go Wrong

    Blessed is the one who is considerate of the destitute:
YHWH will deliver him in the day of evil.
YHWH will protect him and keep him alive;
    he will be blessed in the land;
    he will not be handed over to the desires of his enemies.
YHWH will uphold him even on his sickbed;
    you will transform his bed of illness into health.

As for me,
I said,
    "O YHWH!
    Be gracious to me!
    Heal me!
    For I have sinned against you!"

As for my enemies, with malice they said,
    "When will he die and his name perish?"

As for the one who comes to visit me,
    He speaks lies,
    His heart gathers slander against me.
    He goes around spreading them.

As for all who hate me,
    They whisper together against me;
    They desire to do me harm.
    They say,
        "Wickedness is entrenched in him.
        Once he is brought low,
        he will not rise again."

As for my best friend-
   The one in whom I trusted,
   The one who ate my bread,
  Even he has lifted up his heel against me!
But you,
O YHWH!
Be gracious to me!
Raise me up!
  So that I may pay them back!

In this way I will know:
  That you are pleased with me,
  That my enemies will not shout in triumph over me.

As for me,
  You will maintain my just cause,
  You will cause me to stand in your presence forever.

Blessed be YHWH God of Israel,
  from eternity to eternity.

Amen and amen!

BOOK II (Psalms 42-72)

The First Psalm in the 2nd Scroll introduces the Sons of Korah, who were in charge of composing vocal and instrumental music for the professional singers, choirs, orchestra, and congregational hymns used in public worship.

The inclusion of Korah's descendants in public worship after Korah betrayed Moses is an illustration of amazing grace. Although the founder of their family died under the wrath of God, yet, they found grace in the eyes of YHWH.

The themes explored in this scroll primarily instruct God's people how to cope with the trials of life when trouble seems to overwhelm you. In particular, David struggles with being betrayed by people he thought were his friends.

Psalm 42

To the Choir Director: A Torah of the Sons of Korah

Hope in God in Times of Trouble

    As an antelope pants for streams of water,
        so my soul pants for you,
           my God!

My soul thirsts for God,
For-
    the living God.
When may I come and appear in God's presence?

My tears have been my food day and night,
    while people keep asking me all day long,
        "Where is your God?"

These things I will recall as I pour out my soul within me:
I used to go with the crowd in a procession to the house of God,
    accompanied with shouts of joy and thanksgiving.

Why are you in despair, O my soul?
Why are you disturbed within me?
Hope in God!
    For once again I will praise him,
        since he is my saving presence.

O my God!
My soul is bowed down within me;
    therefore I will remember you
        from the land of Jordan,
           from the heights of Hermon,
                even from the foothills.

Deep calls to deep at the roar of your waterfalls;
  All your breakers and your waves swirled over me.

By day YHWH will command his gracious love,
By night his song is with me—
    a prayer to the God of my life.

I will ask God, my Rock,
   "Why have you forsaken me?
   Why do I go around mourning under the enemy's oppression?"

Like the shattering of my bones are the taunts of my oppressors,
saying to me all day long,
   "Where is your God?"

Why are you in despair, O my soul?
Why are you disturbed within me?
Hope in God!
  For-
    I once again will praise him,
    Since-
       he is my saving presence and my God.

Psalm 43

Hope in God for Times of Trouble

You be my judge,
O God!

Plead my case against an unholy nation;
Rescue me from the deceitful and unjust man.

Since you are the God who strengthens me,
   Why have you forsaken me?
   Why do I go around mourning under the enemy's oppression?"

Send forth your light and your truth
   so they may guide me.
Let them bring me to your holy mountain and to your dwelling places.
Then I will approach the altar of God,
   even to God who is the gladness of my joy.
Then I will praise you with the lyre,

O God, my God!
Why are you in despair, O my soul?
Why are you disturbed within me?
Hope in God!
For I once again will praise him,
   since he is my saving presence and my God.

Psalm 44

To the Choir Director: A Torah of the Sons of Korah

A Prayer in Times of Defeat

> O God!
> We heard it with our ears;
> Our ancestors told us about a deed you did in their day—
> > a long time ago.
>
> With your hand you expelled the nations,
> With your hand established our ancestors.
>
> You afflicted peoples;
> You cast them out.
>
> It was not with their sword that they inherited the land,
> Their own arm did not deliver them.
> But-
> > it was by your power, your strength,
> > by the light of your face;
> > > because-
> > > > you were pleased with them.
>
> You are my king,
> O God!
> Command victories for Jacob.
>
> Through you we will knock down our oppressors;
> Through your name we will tread down those who rise up against us.
> For-
> > I place no confidence in my bow,
> > My sword will not deliver me.

For-
> You delivered us from our oppressors,
> You put to shame those who hate us.

We will praise God all day long;
To your name we will give thanks forever.

Musical Interlude

However-
> You cast us off and put us to shame!
> You did not even march with our armies!
> You made us retreat from our oppressors.
> > (Our enemies ransacked us.)
> You gave us over to be slaughtered like sheep;
> You scattered us among the nations.
> You sold out your people for nothing,
> You made no profit at that price.
> You made us a laughing stock to our neighbors,
> You made us a source of mockery and derision to those around us.
> You made us an object lesson among the nations;
> > people shake their heads at us.

My dishonor remains before me continuously;
The shame on my face covers me completely,
Because-
> > Of the voice of the one who mocks and reviles,
> > Of the enemy and the avenger.

All this came upon us,
Yet-
We did not forsake you,
We have not dealt falsely with your covenant;
Our hearts have not turned away;
Our steps have not swerved from your path.

Nevertheless-
You crushed us in the lair of jackals,
You covered us in deep darkness,

If we had forgotten the name of our God
If we lifted our hands to a foreign god,
    would not God find out?
    Since he knows the secrets of the heart?
For your sake-
We are being killed all day long.
We are thought of as sheep to be slaughtered.

Wake up!
  Are you asleep?
  O sovereign Lord!
  Get up!
  Do not cast us off forever!

Why are you hiding your face?
Why are you ignoring our affliction and oppression?
For-
    we have collapsed in the dust;
    our bodies cling to the ground.

Arise!
Deliver us!
Redeem us according to your gracious love!

Psalm 45

To the Choir Director: An Torah of the Sons of Korah. A love song to the tune of "Lilies"

A Royal Wedding Song

> My heart is overflowing with good news;
> I speak what I have composed to the king;
> my tongue is like the pen of an articulate scribe.
>
> You are the most handsome of Adam's descendants;
>   grace has anointed your lips;
>   therefore God has blessed you forever.
>
> Strap on your sword to your side,
> O mighty warrior!
> Along with your honor and majesty.
>
> In your majesty ride forth for the cause of truth, humility, and righteousness;
> Your strong right hand will teach you awesome things.
> Your arrows are sharpened to penetrate the hearts of the king's enemies.
> People will fall under you.
>
> "Your throne, O God, is forever and ever,
> The scepter of your kingdom is a righteous scepter.
> You love justice and hate wickedness.
> That is why God, even your God, has anointed you rather than your companions
> with the oil of gladness.
> All your clothes are scented with myrrh, aloes, and cassia.
> From ivory palaces stringed instruments have made you glad.
> The king's daughters are among your honorable women;

the queen, dressed in gold from Ophir, has taken her place at
your right hand."

Listen, daughter!
Consider and pay attention.
Forget your people and your father's house,
the king will greatly desire your beauty.
Because-
    he is your master.
    You should bow in respect before him.
The daughter of Tyre will come with a wedding gift;
wealthy people will entreat your favor.

In her chamber,
    the king's daughter is glorious;
    her clothing is embroidered with gold thread.
In embroidered garments she is presented to the king.
Her virgin companions who follow her train will be presented
to you.
With joy and gladness they are presented as they enter the
king's palace.

Your sons will take the place of your fathers,
You will set them up as princes in all the earth.

From generation to generation,
I will cause your name to be remembered.
Therefore-
    people will thank you forever and ever.

Psalm 46

To the Choir Director: A song by the Sons of Korah, to the tune of "The Maidens"

God is the Refuge of His People

God is our refuge and strength-
    a great help in times of distress.
Therefore-
we will not be frightened
    when the earth roars,
    when the mountains shake in the depths of the seas,
    when its waters roar and rage,
    when the mountains tremble despite their pride.

Musical Interlude

    Lo!
    A river-
        whose streams make the city of God rejoice,
            even the Holy Place of the Most High.

    Since God is in her midst,
        she will not be shaken.
    God will help her at the break of dawn.

    The nations roared;
    The kingdoms were shaken.

    His voice boomed;
      the earth melts.

    YHWH of the Heavenly Armies is with us;
    our refuge is the God of Jacob.

Musical Interlude

> Come!
> Observe the mighty works of YHWH,
> > He causes desolations in the earth.
> > He causes wars to cease all over the earth,
> > He causes the bow to break, the spear to snap,
> > He causes the chariots to burn in fire.
>
> Stand in awe and know that I am God:
> > I will be exalted among the nations.
> > I will be exalted throughout the earth.
>
> YHWH of the Heavenly Armies is with us;
> > the God of Jacob is our refuge.

Musical Climax

Psalm 47

To the Choir Director: A song by the Sons of Korah

YHWH is the Sovereign Ruler over the Nations

> Clap your hands,
> > all you peoples!
> Shout to God with a loud cry of joy!
>
> For-
> YHWH, the Most High, is to be feared,
> He is a great king over all the earth.
> He subdued peoples under us,
> He subdued nations under our feet.
> He chose our inheritance for us,
> > even the pride of Jacob- whom he loved.

Musical Interlude

> God has ascended on high with a shout,
> > even YHWH with the blast of a trumpet.
>
> Sing songs to God;
> Yes, sing songs!
>
> Sing songs to our King;
> Yes, sing songs!
>
> Indeed-
> > God is the sovereign king over the earth;
> > Yes, sing a song of praise.
> > God is sovereign king over the nations;
> > God is seated on his holy throne.
>
> The nobles among the nations have joined the people of the

God of Abraham.
For the shields of the earth belong to God;
   he is greatly exalted.

Psalm 48

A song: Lyrics by the Sons of Korah

Zion, City of our God

    Great is YHWH!
    For-
        he is to be praised greatly,
            even in the city of our God,
                his holy mountain.
    Beautifully situated,
        the joy of all the earth,
        Mount Zion towards the north,
            the city of the great King.
    Within her citadels,
        God is known as a place of refuge.

    Behold-
        when the kings assembled together,
        when they passed over together,
        they looked and were awestruck;
        they became afraid and ran away.
        Trembling seized them there,
            pains like those of a woman in labor,
                as when an east wind destroyed the ships of Tarshish.

    Just as we have heard,
        so have we seen;
    In the city of YHWH of the Heavenly Armies—
        even in the city of our God.
    God will establish her forever.

Musical Interlude

O God!
We have meditated on your gracious love in the midst of your temple.

O God!
According to your name,
so is your praise to the ends of the earth.
Your right hand is filled with righteousness.

Mount Zion will be glad;
The towns of Judah will rejoice because of your judgments.

March around Zion;
   Encircle her;
Count her towers.
   Take note of her ramparts;
Investigate her citadels;
   that you may tell it to the next generation.
For-
   this God is our God forever and ever.
He will guide us until death.

Psalm 49

To the Choir Director: A song by the Sons of Korah

The Destiny of the Wicked and the Righteous Contrasted

Listen to this!
All you people!

Pay attention!
All you who live in the world,
   both average people and those of means,
     the rich and the poor together.

My mouth will speak wisdom,
The meditation of my heart will consist of understanding.
I will focus my attention on a proverb;
I will use the harp to expound my riddle.

Why should I be afraid-
   when evil days come my way,
   when the wickedness of those who deceive me
   surrounds me—
     those who put confidence in their wealth,
     those who boast about their great riches?

No man can redeem the soul of another.
No one can give to God a sufficient payment for him—
For-
   it would cost too much to redeem his life,
   the payments would go on forever—
that-
   he should go on living
   he would not see corruption.

Indeed-
he will see-
>   wise people die;
>   the stupid and the senseless will meet their doom,
>   they will leave their wealth to others.
>   Their tombs are their homes forever;
>   their dwellings from generation to generation.
>   They even name their lands after themselves.

But-
>   Humanity cannot last, despite its conceit;
>   Man shall pass away just like the animals.
>   This is the fate-
>   of those who are foolish
>   of those who approved their words after them.

Musical Interlude

Like sheep-
>   they are destined for the afterlife,
>   with death as their shepherd.

The upright will have dominion over them in the morning;
>   their strength will be consumed in the afterlife,
>   so that they have no home.
God will truly redeem me from the power of the afterlife.
He will surely receive me!

Musical Interlude

Do not be afraid-
>   when someone gets rich,
>   when the glory of his household increases.
>   When he dies-
>   he will not be able to take it all with him—
>   his glory will not descend after him,

although he considers himself blessed while he is alive.

Though people praise you for doing well,
you will end up like your fathers' generation,
never again to see the light of day!

Humanity, despite its conceit,
does not understand that it will perish just like the animals.

Psalm 50

A song of Asaph

The Sacrifices Acceptable to YHWH

> The God of gods!
> YHWH!

> He has spoken.
> He has summoned the earth,
>   from the rising of the sun to its setting place.

> From Zion,
>   the perfection of beauty,
> God has shined forth.

> Our God has appeared.
> He has not been silent;
>   a devouring fire blazed before him,
>   a mighty storm swirled around him.

> He summoned the heavens above and the earth below, to sit in judgment on his
> people, saying,
>   "Assemble before me,
>   O my saints,
>   who have entered into my covenant by sacrifice."
> The heavens revealed his justice,
> For-
>   God is himself the judge.

Musical Interlude

> "Listen!
> O my people!

I am making a pronouncement:
  "O Israel, I, God, your God, am testifying against you.
  I do not rebuke you because of your sacrifices;
  Indeed- your burnt offerings are continually before me.
  I will no longer accept a sacrificial bull from your house;
  I will no longer accept goats from your pens.
  Indeed-
      every animal of the forest is already mine;
      even the cattle on a thousand hills.
      I even know all the birds in the mountains.
  Indeed-
      everything that moves in the field is mine.
  If I were hungry-
      I would not tell you;
      For- the world is mine along with everything in it.
      Why then should I eat the flesh of oxen or drink the
      blood of goats?"

  Offer to God a thanksgiving of praise;
  Pay your vows to the Most High who promised:
      "Call on me in the day of distress.
      I will deliver you,
      You will glorify me."

  As for the wicked, God says,
    "How dare you recite my statutes
    or take my covenant on your lips!
    You hate Torah and toss my words behind you.
    When you see a thief-
        you befriend him,
        you keep company with adulterers.
        you give your mouth free reign for evil,
        your tongue devises deceit.
        you sit and speak against your brother;
        you slander your own mother's son.

These things you did,
  and I kept silent because-
    you assumed that I was like you.
But-
    now I am going to rebuke you,
    I will set forth my case before your very own eyes."

Consider this!
    You who have forgotten God,
    lest I tear you in pieces and there be no deliverer:
    Whoever offers a sacrifice of thanksgiving glorifies me, I will reveal the salvation of God to whomever continues in my way."

Psalm 51

To the Choir Director: A song of David. When the prophet Nathan came to him and rebuked him for his sin.

A Cry for Forgiveness

    Have mercy!
    O God!
    According to your gracious love.

    According to your unlimited compassion,
        Erase my transgressions.
        Wash me from my iniquity,
        Cleanse me from my sin.
            For-
                I acknowledge my transgression,
                my sin is continually before me.
    Against you- you only:
        I have sinned,
        I have done what was evil in your sight.

    As a result-
        you are just in your pronouncement
        you are clear in your judgment.

    Indeed-
        in iniquity I was brought forth;
        in sin my mother conceived me.

    Indeed-
        you are pleased with truth in the inner person,
        you will teach me wisdom in my innermost parts.

    Purge me with hyssop,
        Then I will be clean.

Wash me,
>   Then I will be whiter than snow.

Let me know joy and gladness;
let the bones that you have broken rejoice.

Hide your countenance from my sins.
Erase the record of my iniquities.

O God!
Create a pure heart in me,
Renew a right attitude within me.

Do not cast me from your presence;
Do not take your Holy Spirit from me.
Restore to me the joy of your salvation.

Let a willing spirit take hold of me.
Then-
>   I will teach transgressors about your ways,
>   Sinners will turn to you.

Deliver me from the guilt of shedding blood,
O God!
The God of my salvation!
Then- my tongue will sing about your righteousness.

O sovereign Lord!
Open my lips-
My mouth will declare your praise.

Indeed-
>   you do not delight in sacrifices,
>   or I would give them,
>   you do not desire burnt offerings.

The sacrifices of God are-
    a broken spirit;
    a broken and chastened heart.

O God!
    You will not despise them.

Show favor to Zion in your good pleasure;
Rebuild the walls of Jerusalem.

Then you will be pleased-
    with right sacrifices,
    with burnt offerings,
    with whole burnt offerings.

Then they will offer bulls on your altar.

Psalm 52

To the Choir Director: A song of David about Doeg, the Edomite, when he betrayed him to Saul, saying, "David went to the house of Abimelech."

A Rebuke to Deceitful People

> Why do you boast in evil,
> O mighty one?
> God's gracious love continues.

> Your tongue,
> > like a sharp razor,
> devises wicked things
> It works treachery.

> You love-
> > evil rather than good,
> > falsehood rather than speaking uprightly.

Musical Interlude

> You love all words that devour,
> O deceitful tongue!
> But-
> > God:
> > > will tear you down forever;
> > > will take you away,
> > > will snatch you out of your tent!
> > > will uproot you from the land of the living.

Musical Interlude

> The righteous-
> > will fear when they see this,

will laugh at him, saying,
> "Look, here is a young man who refused to make God
> his strength; instead, he trusted in his great wealth
> and made his wickedness his strength."

But-
> I am like a green olive tree in the house of God;
> I trust in the gracious love of God forever and ever.
> I will praise you forever because of what you did;
> I will proclaim that your name is good in the midst of your faithful ones.

Psalm 53

To the Choir Director: Upon machalat. A song of David.

The Fool and God's Response

> Fools say within themselves,
> > "There is no God."
> They are corrupt and commit iniquity;
> not one of them practices what is good.
>
> God looks down from the heavens upon humanity to see:
> > if anyone showed discernment;
> > if anyone seeks God.
> But-
> > all have fallen away;
> > together they have become corrupt;
> > no one practices what is good, not even one.
>
> Will those who do evil ever learn?
> > They devour my people like they devour bread,
> > They never call on God.
> There they were seized with terror,
> > when there was nothing to fear.
> For God has scattered the bones of those who laid siege against you—
> > you put them to shame,
> > > for God has rejected them.
>
> Would that Israel's deliverance come out of Zion!
> When God restores the fortunes of his people,
> > Jacob will rejoice and Israel will be glad.

Psalm 54

To the Choir Director: With stringed instruments. A song of David about the Ziphites who betrayed him by telling Saul, "David is hiding among us, is he not?"

A Prayer in Times of Trouble

> O God!
>> By your name deliver me!
>> By your power vindicate me!
>
> O God!
>> Listen to my prayer!
>> Please pay attention to the words of my mouth.
>>> For-
>>>> the arrogant have arisen against me;
>>>> the oppressors have sought to take my life.
>>>> They do not keep God in mind!

Musical Interlude

> Behold-
>> God is my helper.
>
> The sovereign Lord is with those who guard my life.
> He will turn back the evil upon those who lie in wait for me.
> In your faithfulness, cut them off.
>
> With a voluntary offering-
>> I will sacrifice to you;
>> I will give thanks to your name,
> O YHWH!

It is good:
> For-
>> he has delivered me from every trouble,
>> my eyes have seen the end of my enemies.

Psalm 55

To the Choir Director: With stringed instruments. A song of David.

Betrayal by a Friend

    Pay attention to my prayer,
    O God!

    Do not hide yourself from my appeal!
    Pay attention to me!
    Answer me!

    I moan and groan in my thoughts because:
        of the voice of the enemy,
        of the oppression of the wicked.

    They bring down evil upon me.
    In anger, they hate me.

    My heart is trembling within me,
    The terrors of death have assaulted me.
    Fear and trembling have overwhelmed me,
    Horror has covered me.
    I said,
        "O, who will give me the wings of a dove,
          so that I could fly away and live somewhere else?"

    Look!
    I want to flee far away.
    I want to settle down in the wilderness.

Musical Interlude

I want to deliver myself quickly from this windstorm and tempest."
Swallow them up!
O sovereign Lord!

Confuse their tongues,
   Because-
      I have seen violence and strife in the city.
Day and night they prowl around its walls;
   evil and iniquity are within it.
Wickedness is at the center of it;
   fraud and lies never leave its streets.
 For-
   it is not an enemy who insults me;
   I could have handled that.
   It is not someone who hates me,
   who now arises against me;
   I could have hidden myself from him.
 But-
   it is you:
     a man whom I treated as my equal;
      my personal confidant,
      my close friend!

We had good fellowship together.
We even walked together in the house of God!

Let death seize them!
May they be plunged alive into the afterlife,
   For-
     gross wickedness is at home among them.

I call upon God,
YHWH will deliver me!
Morning, noon, and night,
I mulled over these things.

I cried out in my distress,
  he heard my voice.
He calmly ransomed my soul from the war waged against me,
  For-
    there was a vast crowd who stood against me.

God will hear me;
  He will humble them;
    The One who dwells on high from of old.

Musical Interlude

  Because-
    they do not repent,
    they do not fear God.

Each of my friends raises his hand against those at peace with them;
Each of my friends breaks his word.
  His mouth is as smooth as butter,
    while war is in his heart.
His words were as smooth as olive oil,
  while his sword is drawn.

Cast on YHWH whatever he sends your way,
  and he will sustain you.
He will never allow the righteous to be shaken.

But-
  you,
  O God,
  will bring them down into the afterlife;
These bloodthirsty and deceitful people will not live out half their days.

In contrast,

I will put my full confidence in you.

Psalm 56

To the Choir Director: A special Psalm of David to the tune of "A Silent Dove Far Away," when the Philistines seized him in Gath.

Trust in God When Betrayed By Man

    Have mercy on me!
    O God!
    Because men have harassed me.

    Those who oppress me have fought against me all day long.
    Those who watch me all day have harassed me,
    For-
        there are many who fight against me out of conceit.

    On days when I am afraid I put my ultimate confidence in you.
    In God-
        I will praise his word.
    In God-
        I will put my full confidence.
        I will not fear what mere man can do to me.

    All day long they distort what I say;
    All their schemes against me are for evil purposes.
    They gather together;
    They hide in ambush.
    They watch my every step as they lie in wait for my life.

    Cast them away because of their wickedness.
    In your wrath,
    O God!
    Cast down these people!

    You have kept count of my wanderings.
    You put my tears in your bottle—

Have you not recorded them in your book?

My enemies will retreat when I cry to you.
This has been my experience,
Because-
  God is with me.

In God-
  I will praise his word;

In YHWH-
  I will praise his word.

In God-
  I will put my trust.

I will not fear what mere man can do to me.

  O God!
  I have taken vows before you;
  Therefore-
      I will offer thanksgiving sacrifices to you.
  Because-
      you have delivered me from death
      you have kept my feet from stumbling,
          so that I may walk before God in the light of the living!

Psalm 57

To the Choir Director: A special Psalm of David to the tune "Do Not Destroy," when he fled from Saul into a cave.

A Prayer for Deliverance

> Have mercy on me!
> O God!
> Have mercy!
> In you I have placed my full confidence.
>
> In the shadow of your wings,
> I will find my refuge until this calamity passes.
>
> I call upon the God Most High;
> To the God who completes what he began in me.
> He will send help from heaven to deliver me
>   from those who harass and despise me.

Musical Interlude

> God will send his gracious love and truth.
> I am surrounded by lions.
> I lie down with those who burn with fire;
>   with people whose teeth are like spears and arrows;
>   with people whose tongues are like sharp swords.
>
> Be exalted above the heavens!
> O God!
> May your glory cover the earth!
>
> They have set a snare for my feet,
>   which makes me depressed.
> They dug a pit in front of me,
>   But-

they are the ones who fell into it.

Musical Interlude

    My heart is committed!
    O God!
    My heart is committed!
     I will sing;
     I will play music.

    Wake up!
    My soul!

    Wake up!
    My lyre and harp!

    I will awaken at dawn.
    I will exalt you among the peoples!
    O sovereign Lord!
    I will play music among the nations.
    For-
        your gracious love is great,
        extending even to the heavens,
    For-
        your truth is great,
        extending even to the skies.

    Be exalted above the heavens,
    O God!
    May your glory cover the earth!

Psalm 58

To the Choir Director: A special Psalm of David to the tune "Do Not Destroy"

A Prayer for God's Judgment on His Enemies

Questions for the wicked

> How can you remain silent and speak righteously at the same time?
> How can you judge people fairly?

> As a matter of fact,
>> In your heart you plan iniquities!
>> In the land your hands are violent!

> The wicked go astray from the womb;
> They go astray telling lies even from birth.
> Their venom is like a poisonous snake;
>> like a deaf serpent that shuts its ears,
>>> refusing to hear the voice of the snake charmer
>>> or the cunning enchanter.

> O God!
> Shatter their teeth in their mouths!

> O YHWH!
> Break the fangs of the young lions!
>> May they flow away like rain water that runs off.
>> May they become like someone who shoots broken arrows.
>> May they be like a snail that dries up on its path.
>> May they be like a woman's stillborn baby who never saw the sun.

Before your clay pots are placed on a fire of burning thorns—
>   (whether green or ablaze)
your wrath will sweep them away like a storm.

The righteous person will rejoice:
>   when he sees your vengeance;
>   when he washes his feet in the blood of the wicked.

A person will say,
>   "Certainly, the righteous are rewarded.
>   Certainly, there is a God who judges the earth."

Psalm 59

To the Choir Director: A special Psalm of David to the tune "Do Not Destroy," when Saul sent men to watch the house in order to kill him.

A Prayer for Deliverance and Justice

>Save me from my enemies!
>O my God!
>
>Keep me safe from those who rise up against me.
>Save me from evildoers;
>Deliver me from bloodthirsty men.
>
>Look!
> They lie in ambush for my life;
> These violent men gather together against me,
>   But-
>   not because of any transgression or sin of mine.
>
> O YHWH!
>Without any fault on my part,
> they rush together and prepare themselves.
>
>Get up!
> Come help me!
> Pay attention!
>
>You-
> YHWH God of the Heavenly Armies,
> God of Israel,
> Stir yourself up to punish all the nations.

Show no mercy to those wicked transgressors.

Musical Interlude

At night-
    they return like howling dogs;
    they prowl around the city.

Look what pours out of their mouths!
They use their lips like swords, saying
    "Who will hear us?"

But-
you,
O YHWH!
    You will laugh at them;
    You will mock all the heathen nations.

My Strength!
I will watch for you,
For-
    God is my fortress.

My God of Gracious Love will meet me;
God will enable me to see what happens to my enemies.

Do not kill them,
    lest my people forget.
By your power make them stumble around;
    bring them down low,
O sovereign Lord,
our Shield!

The sin of their mouth is the word on their lips.
    They will be caught in their own conceit;
    They speak curses and lies.

Go ahead and destroy them in anger!
Wipe them out-
    that they will know to the ends of the earth that God rules over Jacob.

Musical Interlude

  At night they return like howling dogs:
    They prowl around the city.
    They scavenge for food.
    If they find nothing,
    they become hungry and growl.

But-
    I will sing of your power
    I will shout for joy in the morning about your gracious love.
For-
    you have been a fortress for me;
    you have been a refuge when I am distressed.
My Strength!
I will sing praises to you,
for you.

O God of Gracious Love,
You are my fortress!

Psalm 60

To the Choir Director: A special Psalm of David to the tune "Lily of The Covenant," for teaching about his battle with Aram-naharaim and Aram-zobah, when Joab returned and attacked 12,000 Edomites in the Salt Valley.

A Prayer for God's Help against his enemies

    O God!
        You have cast us off.
        You have breached our defenses.
        You have become enraged.
    Return to us!

    You made the earth quake;
    You broke it open.
    Repair its fractures,
    Because-
        it has shifted.

    You made your people go through hard times;
    You had us drink wine that makes us stagger.

    But-
        you have given a banner to those who fear you,
            so they may display it in honor of truth.

Musical Interlude

    So your loved ones may be delivered,
    Save us by your power!
    Answer us quickly!

    Then God spoke in his holiness,

"I will rejoice—
I will divide Shechem;
I will portion out the Succoth Valley.
Gilead belongs to me, and Manasseh is mine.
Ephraim is my helmet, and Judah my scepter.
Moab is my wash basin; over Edom I will throw my shoes;
over Philistia I will celebrate my triumph."

Who will lead me to the fortified city?
Who will lead me to Edom?
Are you the One?
O God!
Have you cast us off?

O God!
Are you the One who refused to accompany our armies?

Help us in our distress,
For-
   human help is worthless.

Through God we will fight valiantly;
It is he who will crush our enemies!

Psalm 61

To the Choir Director: A musical composition by David for stringed instruments

A Prayer for God's Protection

> O God!
> Hear my cry!
> Pay attention to my prayer!
>
> From the end of the earth I will cry to you.
> Whenever my heart is overwhelmed,
> Place me on the rock that would normally be too high for me.
> For-
> > you have been a refuge for me,
> > you have been a tower of strength before the enemy.
>
> Let me make my home in your tabernacle forever;
> Let me hide under the shelter of your wings.

Musical Interlude

> For-
> You,
> > O God!
> > have heard my promises.
> You,
> > have assigned to me the heritage of those who fear your name.
>
> Add day after day to the king's life;
> May his years continue for many generations.
> May he be enthroned before God forever.
> Appoint your gracious love and truth to guard him.

So-
> I will sing songs to your name forever;
> I will fulfill my promises day by day.

Psalm 62

To the Choir Director: According to the style of Jeduthun. A song of David.

A song of Trust in God

>My soul rests quietly as it looks to God;
>>from him comes my deliverance.
>
>He alone is-
>>my rock,
>>my deliverance,
>>my high tower;
>>nothing will shake me!

>How long will you rage against someone?
>Would you attack him as if he were a leaning wall or a tottering fence?

>They plan to cast him down from his exalted position.
>They delight in lies:
>>their mouth utters blessings,
>>while their heart is cursing.

Musical Interlude

>My soul,
>be quiet before God,
>for-
>>from him comes my hope.
>
>He alone is:
>>my rock,
>>my deliverance,
>>my high tower;
>>nothing will shake me!

On God my deliverance and my glory rests;
   my strong rock—
   my refuge—
   is in God.

O people,
   in every situation-
      put your full confidence in him;
      pour out your heart before him;
      for-
         God is a refuge for us.

Musical Interlude

Common people are often empty and void,
But-
People in high positions are not what they appear:
   When they are placed on the scales,
      they weigh nothing;
      even when weighed together,
      they are less than nothing.

Do not trust in oppression;
   since stealing is a false hope.
If you become wealthy,
   do not set your heart on that illusion.

God spoke once,
But-
   I heard it twice,
      "Power belongs to God."
Also to you,
O sovereign Lord,
belongs gracious love,
because-
   you reward each person according to his work.

Psalm 63

A song of David, while he was hiding in the Judean wilderness.

Joyful Trust in God

    O God!
    You are my God!

    I will fervently seek you.
    My soul thirsts for you;
    My flesh longs for you in a dry, weary, and parched land.
    So I have looked for you in the sanctuary,
        to behold your power and glory.
    Because your gracious love is better than life itself,
        my lips shall praise you.
    So-
        I will bless you as long as I live;
        I will lift up my hands in your name.

    Just as I am satisfied with the choicest of foods,
        the lips of my mouth will praise you joyfully.

    When I think of you while lying in bed,
        I will meditate on you in the night watches.
    For-
        you have been my strength,
    In the shadow of your wings,
    I will shout for joy.

    My soul clings to you,
        even as your right hand supports me.

    But-
        as for those seek to destroy me,
            they will go down into the depths of the earth;

>   they will be given over to the power of the sword;
>   they will become carrion for jackals.
> But-
> as for the king,
>   he will rejoice in God.
>
> Indeed-
>   everyone who swears by him will exult,
>   because-
>   the mouths of liars will be silenced.

Psalm 64

To the Choir Director: A song of David.

A Prayer for Protection

Hear!
O God!
 As I express my concern:
  "Protect me from the enemy that I fear.
   Hide me from the secret plots of the wicked,
   Hide me from the mob of evildoers;
    who sharpen their tongues like swords,
    who aim their bitter words like arrows,
     shooting at the innocent in ambush."

Suddenly they shoot,
 fearing nothing:
  They concoct an evil scheme for themselves;
  They enumerate their hidden snares;
  They say, "Who will see them?"
  They devise wicked schemes, saying,
   "We have completed our plans,
    hiding them deep in our hearts."

But-
 God shot an arrow at them:
  They were wounded immediately,
  They tripped over their own tongues.

  Everyone who was watching ran away.
  Everyone was gripped with fear.
  Everyone acknowledged God's deeds.
  Everyone understood what he had done.

The righteous rejoiced in YHWH,

Because-
they had fled to him for refuge.
Let all the upright in heart glorify God.

Psalm 65

To the Choir Director: A song with Lyrics by David.

A song of Praise to God

    In Zion-
    O God!
    Praise silently awaits you.
    The vow will be paid to you.

    Since you hear prayer,
        —everybody will come to you.
    My acts of iniquity
        —they overwhelm me!
    Our transgressions
        —you blot them out!

    How blessed is the one whom you choose,
        the one you cause to come into your courts!

    We will be satisfied with the goodness of your house,
    Yes-
    We will be satisfied even with the holiness of your temple.

    With awesome deeds of justice
      you will answer us,
    O God our Deliverer!
      You are the confidence for all those:
        who dwell at the ends of the earth,
        who live by the sea far away.

He who established the mountains by his strength is clothed with omnipotence.
He can calm:
> the roar of seas,
> the roaring of the waves,
> the turmoil of the peoples.

Those living at the furthest ends of the earth are seized by fear because of your miraculous deeds.

You make the going forth of the morning and the evening shout for joy.
You take care of the earth.
You water it.
You enrich it greatly with the river of God that overflows with water.
You provide grain for them.
You have ordained it.
You fill the furrows of the field with water so that their ridges overflow.
You dissolve them with rain showers.
You have blessed their sprouts.
You crown the year with your goodness.
Your footsteps drop prosperity behind them.

The wilderness pastures drip with dew.
The hills wrap themselves with joy.
The meadows are clothed with flocks of sheep.
The valleys are covered with grain.
> They shout for joy.
> Yea-
> They burst out in song!

Psalm 66

To the Choir Director: A song of Praise

Shout praise to God all the earth!
Sing praise about the glory of his name!
Make his praise glorious!

Say to God:
> "How awesome are your works!
> Because of your great strength
> your enemies will cringe before you.
> The whole earth worships you.
> They sing praise to you.
> They sing praise to your name. "

Musical Interlude

Come and see the awesome works of God on behalf of human beings:
> He turned the sea into dry land.
> Israel crossed the river on foot.

Let us rejoice in him.

He rules by his power forever,
His eyes are watching over the nations.
Do not let rebellious people exalt themselves.

Musical Interlude

Bless our God!
O you people!
Let the sound of his praise be heard.
> "He gives us life
> He does not permit our feet to slip."

For-
you-
O God!
    You have tested us to purify us like fine silver.
    You have led us into a trap.
    You have set burdens on our backs.
    You caused men to ride over us.
    You brought us through fire and water.

    But-
    You also led us to abundance!

    I will come to your house with burnt offerings.
    I will fulfill my vows to you:
        that my lips uttered,
        that my mouth spoke,
        when I was in trouble.
    I will offer to you:
        burnt offerings of fat,
        along with the smoke of the sacrifice of rams.
    I will offer bulls along with goats.

Musical Interlude

    Come!
    Listen to me!,
    All of you who fear God,
    so that I will tell you what he did for me.
        "I called aloud to him,
        I praised him with my tongue.
        Were I to cherish iniquity in my heart,
        O sovereign Lord,
        you would not listen to me.
        Surely God has heard,
        and he paid attention to my prayers."

Blessed be God!
>   He did not turn away my prayers.
>   He did not turn away his gracious love from me.

Psalm 67

To the Choir Director: Accompanied by stringed instruments. A Psalm.

Thanksgiving Be To God

   May God show us favor and bless us!
   May he truly show us his favor!

Musical *Interlude*

   Let your ways be known by all the nations of the earth,
      along with your deliverance.
   Let the people thank you,
   O God!
   Let all the people thank you.
   Let the nations rejoice;
   Let the nations sing for joy,
      because you judge people with fairness
         and you govern the people of the earth.

Musical Interlude

   Let the people thank you,
   O God!
   Let all the people thank you.

   May the earth yield its produce.
   May God, our God,
   Bless us!
   May God truly bless us so that all the peoples of the earth will fear him.

Psalm 68

To the Choir Director: A Psalm.

Praise to God

>When God arises,
>>his enemies are scattered.
>
>Those who hate him,
>>Flee from his presence:
>>>As smoke is driven away,
>>>>so you drive them away.
>>>
>>>As wax melts in the presence of fire,
>>>>so the wicked die in the presence of God.
>
>But-
>>>the righteous rejoice,
>>>the righteous exult before God;
>>>the righteous are overwhelmed with joy.
>
>Sing to God!
>Sing praises to his name!
>Exalt the one who rides on the clouds!

YHWH is his name!

>Be jubilant in his presence.
>As a father is to orphans and an advocate to widows is God in his holy dwelling place.
>
>God causes the lonely to dwell in families.
>He leads prisoners into prosperity,
>But-
>>rebels will live on parched land.
>
>O God!
>When you led out your people,
>When you marched through the desert, the land quaked.

Musical *Interlude*

    Indeed-
        the heavens poured down rain from the presence of God,
        this God of Sinai,
            from the presence of God,
            the God of Israel.

    O God!
    You poured out abundant rain on your inheritance.

    When Israel was weary,
        you sustained her.

    Your people live there;
    You sustain the needy with your goodness,
    O God!
    The Sovereign Lord gave the Word,
        and numerous were the women who proclaimed it:
            "Kings of armies retreat and flee,
                while the lady of the house divides the spoil!
                When young men lie down among the sheepfolds,
                      you are like the wings of the dove covered with silver,
                          with its feathers in glittering gold."

    When the Almighty scattered the kings there,
        there was snow on Mt. Zalmon.
    The mountain of God is:
        as the mountain of Bashan;
        as a mountain of many peaks is Mount Bashan.
    O you mountains of many peaks,
    why do you watch with envy the mountain in which God has
        chosen to dwell?

    Indeed-

YHWH will live there forever.

God's chariots were many thousands.
The sovereign Lord was there with them at Sinai in holiness.
   You ascended to the heights,
   You took captives.
   You received gifts among mankind,
     even the rebellious,
So YHWH God may live there.

Blessed be the sovereign Lord who daily carries us.
God is our deliverer!

Musical *Interlude*

   God is for us!
   Even the God of our deliverance.

   YHWH the sovereign Lord rescues us from death.
   God surely strikes the heads of his enemies,
     even the hairy heads of those who continue in their guilt.

   The sovereign Lord says,
    "I will bring them from Bashan,
     I will bring them from the depths of the sea,
      So that your feet may wade through their blood.
     The tongues of your dogs will have their portions from your enemies."

They have observed your processions,
  O God!
The processions of my God,
The processions of my king in the sanctuary.
The singers are in front,
The musicians follow,
   strumming their stringed instruments

among the maidens who are playing their tambourines.

Bless God in the great congregation,
YHWH who is the fountain of Israel.

Little Benjamin is there,
   leading them.
   leading:
      the princes of Judah;
      the princes of Zebulun;
      the princes of Naphtali.

Summon the power of your God!
The sovereign power that you have shown us.
O God!
Because of your temple in Jerusalem,
   kings bring tribute to you.

Rebuke:
   the wildlife that lives among the reeds,
   the nations that congregate like bulls and cows,
      humbling themselves with pieces of silver,
         for God scatters the nations that delight in battle.
   Envoys will come from Egypt.
Let the Ethiopians stretch out their hands to God.
O you kingdoms of the earth:
   Sing to God!
   Sing praises to the sovereign Lord!

Musical *Interlude*

To the one who rides the heavens,
   the ancient heavens.

Behold!
He thunders with a mighty voice.

Ascribe sovereign power to this God,
    whose glory is over Israel,
    whose power is in the skies.

You are awesome,
O God!
Even from your sanctuaries.

The God of Israel is the One who gives strength and power to the people.

Blessed be God!

Psalm 69

To the Choir Director: A composition of David set to the tune: "The Lilies"

A Cry For Divine Deliverance

    Deliver me!
    O God!
        Because:
            The waters are up to my neck.
            I am sinking in deep mire,
            There is no solid ground.
            I have come into deep water,
            The flood overwhelms me.
            I am exhausted from calling for help.
            My throat is parched.
            My eyes are strained from looking for God.
            Those who hate me without cause are more than the hairs of my head.
            My persecutors are mighty,
            They want to destroy me.

    Must I be forced to return what I did not steal?
    O God!

    You know my sins,
    My guilt is not hidden from you.
    Do not let those who look up to you be ashamed because of me.

    YHWH the sovereign Lord of the Heavenly Armies!
    Let not those who seek you be humiliated because of me.

    O God of Israel!

I am being mocked because of you.
Dishonor overwhelms me.
I am a stranger to my brothers,
I am a foreigner to my mother's sons.

Zeal for your house consumes me,
The mockeries of those who insult you fall on me.

I weep!
I fast!
I am mocked for it.

When I dressed in sackcloth,
    I became an object of gossip among them.
The prominent people mock me,
    composing drinking songs.

But-
  As for me,
O YHWH!
  May my prayer to you come at a favorable time.

O God!
In the abundance of your gracious love,
    Answer me with your sure deliverance.
    Rescue me from the mud!
    Do not let me sink down in it.
    Rescue me from those who hate me,
    Rescue me from the deep waters.
    Do not let the floodwaters overwhelm me
    Do not let the deep swallow me up,
    Do not let the mouth of the well close over me.
Answer me!
O YHWH!
Your gracious love is good;
Therefore turn to me in keeping with your great compassion.

Do not ignore your servant because I am in great distress.
Hurry to answer me!
Draw near to me!
Redeem me!
Ransom me because of my enemies.

Truly you know my reproach, shame, and disgrace.
All my enemies are known to you.

Insults broke my heart.
I despaired;
I looked for sympathy, but there was none,
I looked for comforters, but I found none.
They put poison in my food,
In my thirst they forced me to drink vinegar.
May their dining tables:
    entrap them,
    become a snare for their allies.

May their eyes be blinded.
May their bodies tremble continually.
May you pour out your fury on them.
May your burning anger overtake them.
May their camp become desolate,
May their tents remain unoccupied.

For:
    they persecute those whom you have struck,
    they brag about the pain of those you have wounded.

May you punish them for their crimes;
May they receive no verdict of innocence from you.
May they be erased from the Book of Life,
May their names not be written with the righteous.

But as for me—
   I am afflicted and hurting.

O God!
May your deliverance establish me on high.

Let me praise the name of God with a song
    In order that I may magnify him with thanksgiving.
That will please YHWH more than oxen and bulls with horns and hooves.

The afflicted will watch and rejoice.
May you who seek God take courage.
   For:
     YHWH listens to the needy
      YHWH does not despise those in bondage.

Let the heavens and earth praise him,
    along with the sea and its swarming creatures.
 For:
   God will deliver Zion;
    God will rebuild the cities of Judah
      so they may live there and possess them.
    The descendants of his servants will inherit it.
    Those who cherish his name will live there.

Psalm 70

To the Choir Director. A composition of David set to the tune of "A Memorial"

Help me!
O YHWH!

O God!
Come to my rescue!

O YHWH!
Hurry to help me!

May those who seek to kill me be publicly humiliated.
May those who take pleasure in my harm be turned back in humiliation.
May those who say "Aha! Aha!" be turned back because of their shameful deeds.

Let those who seek you greatly rejoice in you.
Let those who love your deliverance say,
    "May God be continually exalted."

As for me,
I am poor and needy!

O God!
Come quickly to me!
For you are my helper and my deliverer.

O YHWH!
Please do not delay!

Psalm 71

A Prayer for YHWH to Deliver Him

O YHWH!
In you I take refuge.

Do not let me be humiliated!
Rescue and deliver me,
    because you are righteous.

Turn your ear to me!
Deliver me!

Be my shelter where I may go continually;
Command my deliverance
    for you are my rock and fortress.

My God!
Deliver me from the power of the wicked.
Deliver me from the grasp of ruthless evildoers.
For you are my only hope!

O YHWH my Sovereign Lord!
You have been my security since I was young.
I depended on you since birth,
    when you brought me from my mother's womb;
I praise you continually.

I have become an example to many
    that you are my strong refuge.
My mouth is filled with your praise and your splendor daily.
Do not throw me away when I am old;
Do not abandon me when my strength fails.

For my enemies talk against me;
Those who seek to kill me plot together,
  saying,
     "God has abandoned him.
      Run after him and seize him,
      because there's no deliverer."
O God!
Do not be distant from me!

O my God!
Come quickly to help me!

Let my adversaries be ashamed and consumed;
Let those who seek my destruction be covered with scorn and disgrace.

But as for me-
  I will hope continually,
  I will praise you more and more,
  I will declare your righteousness,
  I will declare your salvation every day,
     though I do not fully understand
      what the final outcome will be.
O YHWH, my sovereign Lord!
  I will come in the power of your mighty acts,
    remembering your righteousness—
      yours alone.

O God!
You taught me from my youth,
  so I am still declaring your awesome deeds.

O God!
When I reach old age and have gray hair,
Do not forsake me,

until I have declared your power
    to this generation
        and your might to the next one.

O God!
Your many righteous deeds are great.

O God!
Who can compare to you?
Who caused me to experience many distresses and evil?
You will return to revive me.
You will lift me up from the depths of the earth.
You will increase my honor.
You will comfort me once again.

I also will praise you with the harp;
    because of your faithfulness.

My God!
I will praise you with the lyre.

O Holy One of Israel!
My lips will shout for joy
    when I sing praise to you,
        whose life you have redeemed.

Moreover-
    my tongue will speak all day about your justice;
        for those who seek my destruction will be utterly
        humiliated.

Psalm 72

A Composition of King Solomon

May the King Dispense Divine Justice

O God!
Enable the king to dispense your justice!

Enable the king's son to dispense your right decisions.

May he rule your people with right decisions.
May he rule your oppressed ones with justice.
May the mountains bring prosperity to the people.
May the hills bring righteousness.
May he defend the afflicted of the people.
May he deliver the children of the poor,
May he crush the oppressor.
May they fear you as long as the sun and moon shine—
    from generation to generation.
May he be like the rain that descends on mown grass,
    like showers sprinkling on the ground.
  The righteous will flourish at the proper time
    and peace will prevail until the moon is no more.
May he rule from sea to sea,
    from the Euphrates River to the ends of the earth.
May the nomads bow down before him,
May his enemies lick the dust.
May the kings of Tarshish and of distant shores bring gifts,
May the kings of Sheba and Seba offer tribute.
May all kings bow down to him,
May all nations serve him.

For-

He will deliver the needy when they cry out for help,
He will deliver the poor when there is no deliverer.
He will have compassion on the poor and the needy,
He will save the lives of the needy.
He will redeem them from oppression and violence,
 since their lives are precious in his sight.

May he live long and be given gold from Sheba,
May prayer be offered for him continually,
May he be blessed every day.
May grain be abundant in the land piled up to the mountain tops;
May its fruits flourish like the forests of Lebanon,
May the cities sprout like the grass of the earth.
May his fame be as eternal as the sun's,
May his name endure.
May they be blessed through him
May all nations call him blessed.
Blessed be YHWH!
The God of Israel,
Who alone does awesome deeds.
Blessed be his glorious name forever,

May the whole earth be filled with his glory.
Amen and amen!

This ends the prayers of Jesse's son David.

BOOK III (PSALMS 73-89)

This scroll begins with Asaph's musical testimony how he overcame envying the wicked by considering their end. The Psalms, hymns, and songs in Scroll 3 focus on overcoming wrong attitudes toward God. Some Psalms are filled with bitter complaints against God. When things do not go the way you want, there is always the temptation to become bitter against God. These Psalms also deal with bitterness over the heathen nations destroying Jerusalem and its Temple, and allowing the people to go into captivity. The cure for bad attitudes against God is the truth of God's absolute sovereignty over all things. Whatever God ordains is right!

Psalm 73

A song celebrating Asaph's personal experience of how he learned to overcome envying the wicked.

> God is indeed good to Israel,
>> to those pure in heart!
>
> But-
> as for me-
>> my feet nearly stumbled,
>> I almost lost my step.
>
> For-
>> I was envious of the proud
>>> when I observed the prosperity of the wicked:
>
> There is no struggle at their deaths,
> Their bodies are healthy.
> They do not experience problems common to ordinary people;
> They are not afflicted like other people.
> Therefore they wear pride as their necklace and violence is their garment.
> Their eyes bulge from fatness,
> Their imaginations in their heart are wicked.
> Their mockery.
> They speak evil.
> They boast of oppression out of their arrogance.
> They choose to slander against heaven;
> They gossip about things on earth.
>> (God's people turn there and drink it all in like water until they are satiated.)
>
> Then they say,
>> "How can God know?
>> Does the Most High have knowledge?"

Just look at these wicked people!
They are always carefree.
They are always increasing their wealth.

Have I kept my heart pure for nothing?
Have I kept my hands clean from blood guilt?
For I suffer all day long!
I am punished every morning!

If I say,
   "I will talk like this,"
I would betray a generation of your children!

When I tried to understand this,
   it was too difficult for me
But when I entered the sanctuaries of God,
Then I understood their destiny.

You have certainly set them in slippery places;
You will make them fall to their ruin.
How desolate they quickly become when overtaken by unforeseen calamities.

O YHWH!
Like a dream when one awakens,
You will despise them when you arise.

When I chose to be bitter-
I was emotionally pained.
But then,
I was too stupid to realize I was like a wild beast before you.

But now,
I am always with you.

You are holding me by my right hand.

You will guide me in life with your wise counsel,
After that you will take me up with honor.
After all-
    whom do I have in heaven but you?
I desire nothing on this earth.

My body and mind may fail,
but God is my strength and my portion forever.

Those far from you will perish;
You will destroy those who are unfaithful to you.

As for me,
how good it is for me that God is near!
I have made YHWH the sovereign Lord my refuge,
I can thus publicly tell others about all your deeds.

Psalm 74

A Maskil of Asaph about the destruction of the nation and hope for restoration.

May YHWH remember us!

>Why God?
>Why have you rejected us forever?
>Why is your anger burning against the sheep of your pasture?
>
>Remember your covenant community,
>   whom you redeemed long ago,
>   the tribe whom you redeemed
>   for your personal possession.
>Remember Mount Zion,
>   where you live.
>
>Hurry!
>Look at the permanent ruins—
>   every calamity the enemy brought upon the holy place.
>
>Those opposing you give a battle cry in the very place we meet
>   with you in worship!
>They unfurl their war banners as signs.
>As one blazes a trail through a forest with an ax,
>They are now tearing down all its carved work with hatchets and hammers.
>They burned your sanctuary to the ground,
>   desecrating your dwelling place.
>They say to themselves,
>   "We will crush them completely;"
>They burned down all the meeting places of God in the land.
>
>We see no divine signs around us;
>There is no longer a prophet.

No one among us knows the future.

O God!
How long will the adversary scorn us?
How long will the enemy despise your name?
Forever?
Why don't you withdraw your hand—
    your right hand of power--
from your bosom,
And destroy them?

As for me,
God is my king from ancient times.

You work deliverance throughout the earth.
You split the sea by your sovereign power.
You shattered the heads of sea monsters in the water.
You crushed the heads of the Leviathan.
You set it as food for desert creatures.
You opened both the spring and the river;
You dried up flowing rivers.
Yours is the day, and yours is the night;
You established the moon and the sun.
You set all the boundaries of the earth;
You made summer and winter.

Remember this:
The enemy scorns YHWH;
They despise your name - like fools!

Do not hand over the life of your dove to the beasts;
Do not continually forget your afflicted ones.

Pay attention to your covenant,
    for the dark regions of the earth are full of violence.

Do not let the oppressed return in humiliation.
The poor and needy will praise your name.

Rise up!
O God!
Prosecute your case against them!
Remember that you are being mocked by these fools all day
 long.

Do not ignore the taunts of those opposing you.
Do not ignore the roaring of those who rebel against you
 continuously.

Psalm 75

To the Choir Director: To the tune "Do not Destroy!"
A Psalm of Asaph.

O God!
We praise you,
We praise you in your presence
We draw near as we declare your wonderful deeds.

"At the time that I choose
I will judge the righteous.
While the earth and all its inhabitants melt away,
it is I who keeps its pillars firm."

Musical *Interlude*

I will say to the proud,
"Do not brag."
I will say to the wicked,
"Do not vaunt your strength.
Do not use your strength to fight heaven
Do not speak from stubborn arrogance."

Exaltation comes not:
from the East,
from the West,
from the wilderness.
Since God is the judge,
He will debase this one or that one he will exalt.
For there is a cup in the hand of YHWH,
foaming with well-mixed wine
He will pour it out,
leaving only the dregs,
all the wicked of the earth shall drink it.

But as for me,
I will declare forever,
I will sing praise to the God of Jacob.
I will destroy the vaunted strength of the wicked,
    but the strength of the righteous will be established.

Psalm 76

To the Choir Director: With stringed instruments. A Psalm of Asaph.

Our God is a God of War!

>God is known in Judah;
>His reputation is great in Israel.
>
>His abode is in Salem,
>His dwelling place in Zion.
>There he shattered sharp arrows, shields, swords, and weapons of war.

Musical *Interlude*

>You are robed with light;
>>more majestic than mountains filled with game.
>
>Brave men were plundered
>>while they slumbered in their sleep.
>
>All the men of the army were immobilized.
>
>O God of Jacob!
>At the sound of your battle cry,
>both horse and chariot rider fell into deep sleep.
>
>You are awesome!
>Who can stand in your presence when you are angry?
>
>From heaven you declared judgment.
>The earth stands in awe and is quiet when:
>>God arose to execute justice
>>God arose to deliver all the afflicted of the earth.

Musical Interlude

Even man's anger will glorify you;
You will wear the survivors of your wrath as a necklace.

Let everyone who stands before YHWH your God:
Make a vow and fulfill it to the Awesome One.

He will humble arrogant generals,
Instilling fear among the kings of the earth.

Psalm 77

To the Choir Director: To Jeduthun. A Psalm of Asaph.

Remembering God in Times of Trouble

> I cry out to God!
> I cry out to God
> He hears me.
>
> When I was in distress,
>   I sought the sovereign Lord;
>   My hands were raised at night
>   They did not grow weary.
>
> I refused to be comforted.
> When I remember God, I groan
> I meditate,
>   when my spirit grows faint.

Musical *Interlude*

> You kept my eyes open!
> I was troubled,
> I could not speak.
> I thought of ancient times,
> I considered years long past.
>
> During the night
> I remembered my song.
> I meditate in my heart,
> My spirit within me wonders:
>
>   "Will the sovereign Lord reject me forever?
>   Will he never show me favor again?

Has his grace and love for me ceased forever?
Will his promise to me be unfulfilled in future generations?
Has God forgotten to be gracious to me?
Has he in anger withheld his compassion from me?"

Musical Interlude

So I said:
  "It causes me pain that the right hand of the Most High has changed."
Indeed-
  I will remember YHWH's deeds.
  I will remember your awesome deeds from long ago.

  As I meditate on all your works,
  I will consider your awesome deeds.

  O God!
  Your way is holy!
  Who is a God like our great God?
  O God!
  You are the one who does awesome deeds.
  You reveal your sovereign power among the nations.
  You delivered your people—
    the descendants of Jacob and Joseph—
      with your power.

Musical *Interlude*

The waters saw you,
O God!

The waters saw you and tossed to and fro.
Indeed-

The depths of the sea quaked.
The clouds poured rain;
The skies rumbled.

Indeed-
Your lightning bolts flashed.
Your thunder was heard in the whirlwind;
Your lightning lights up the world;
   (the earth becomes agitated and shook)
Your path way was through the sea;
Your path way through mighty waters;
Your footprints cannot be traced.
You have led your people like a flock of sheep by the hands of Moses and Aaron.

Psalm 78

A Maskil of Asaph

God's Mercy and Judgment in history

   Listen!
     O my people,
   To my Torah.

   Hear the words of my mouth.
   And I will tell you a parable:
       speaking riddles from long ago—
       things that we have heard and known
       things that our ancestors related to us.

   We will not withhold them from their descendants;
   We will declare to the next generation-
       the praises of YHWH;
       the great and awesome deeds he has performed.

   He established a decree in Jacob,
   He established the Torah in Israel,
      that he commanded our ancestors to reveal to their children
   in order that the next generation—
     children yet to be born—
     will know them and in turn teach them to their children.

   They will then put their full confidence in God
   They will not forget his awesome deeds.

   Instead-
   They will keep his commandments.

They will not be like the rebellious generation of their ancestors,
A rebellious generation:
>   whose heart was not steadfast,
>   whose spirits were unfaithful to God.

The Ephraimites were sharp shooters with the bow,
They retreated in the day of battle.
They did not keep God's covenant,
They refused to live by his Torah.
They have forgotten what he has done,
>   Even his awesome deeds that they witnessed.

He performed wonderful things:
>   in the presence of their ancestors.
>   in the land of Egypt.
>   in the fields of Zoan.

He divided the sea so that they were able to cross;
He caused the water to stand in a single location.
He led them with a cloud during the day.
He led them during the night with light from the fire.
He caused the rocks to split in the wilderness.
He gave them water as from an abundant sea.
He brought streams from rock,
>   causing water to flow like a river.
But time and again,
>   They sinned against him,
>   They rebelled against the Most High in the desert.
>   >   To test God was in their minds,
>   >   >   when they demanded food to satisfy their cravings.
>   They spoke against God saying,
>   >   "Is God able to prepare a feast in the desert?

>   It is true that Moses struck the rock and water flowed
>   Forth and torrents of water gushed out.
>   But is he also able to give bread
>   or to supply meat for his people?"

Therefore-
   when YHWH heard this,
   he became angry,
       fire broke out against Jacob.

 Moreover-
  his anger flared against Israel,
     because:
         they did not believe in God
           they did not trust in his deliverance.

Yet-
     He commanded the skies above to open.
     He commanded the doors of the heavens to open,
        so that manna rained down on them for food.
     He sent them the grain of heaven.

Mere man ate the food of angels!
He sent provision to them in abundance.

He stirred up the east wind in the heavens.
He drove the south wind by his might.
He caused meat to rain on them like dust
    and winged birds as the sand of the sea.
He caused them to fall in the middle of the camp
    and all around their tents.
So they ate and were very satisfied,
    because he granted their desire.
However-
    before they had fulfilled their desire,
    while their food was still in their mouths,

the anger of God flared against them:
    he killed the strongest men
    he humbled Israel's young men.

In spite of all of this,
    they kept right on sinning
    they did not believe in his awesome deeds.
So-
    he made their days end in futility,
    he filled their years with sudden terror.

When he struck them down:
    they sought him;
    they repented,
    they eagerly sought God.

Then-
    they remembered that God was their Rock,
    they remembered the Most High God was their Deliverer.

But-
    they tried to deceive him with their mouths;
    they lied to him with their tongues.
    their hearts were not really committed to him,
    they were not really faithful to his covenant.

But-
    He is merciful.
    He forgave their iniquity.
    He did not destroy them.
    He restrained his anger.
    He did not vent all his wrath.
    He remembered that they were only dust,
        a passing wind that does not return.

How they rebelled against him in the desert,
    grieving him in the wilderness!
They tested God again and again,
    provoking the Holy One of Israel.
They did not remember his power.
They did not remember the day he delivered them from their adversary,
    when he set his signs in Egypt,
    his wonders in the plain of Zoan.

He turned their rivers into blood,
He made their streams undrinkable.
He sent swarms of insects to bite them
He sent frogs to destroy them.
He gave their crops to caterpillars
    and what they worked for to locusts.
He destroyed their vines with hail
He destroyed their sycamore trees with frost.
He delivered their beasts to hail,
He delivered their livestock to lightning bolts.
He inflicted his burning anger, wrath, indignation, and distress.
He sent destroying angels among them.
He blazed a path for his anger;
He did not stop short from killing them,
He handed them over to pestilence.
He struck every firstborn in Egypt,
    the first fruits of their manhood in the tents of Ham.
Yet-
He led out his people like sheep,
    guiding them like a flock in the desert.
He led them to safety so they would not fear.

As for their enemies-
  the sea covered them.

He brought the people to the border of his holy mountain,
  which he acquired by his might.
He drove out nations before them,
He allotted their tribal inheritance,
    settling the tribes of Israel in their tents.

 But-
    they tested the Most High God by rebelling against him,
    they did not obey his statutes.
    they fell away
    they were as disloyal as their ancestors.
    they became unreliable, like a defective bow;
    they angered him with their high places.
    they made him jealous with their carved images.

 God heard-
    He became furious,
    He completely rejected Israel.
    He abandoned the tabernacle at Shiloh,
        the tent that he established among mankind.
    He sent his "might" into captivity;
    He sent his "glory" into the control of the adversary.
    He delivered his people over to the sword
    He was angry with his possession.

  The young men were consumed by fire,
  The virgins had no marriage celebrations.
  The priests fell by the sword,
  Yet their widows could not weep.

  The sovereign Lord awoke as though from sleep,
    like a mighty warrior stimulated by wine.
  He beat back his adversaries,
    disgracing them forever.
  He rejected the tribe of Joseph;
  He did not choose the tribe of Ephraim.

But he chose the tribe of Judah,
   the mountain of Zion,
      which he loves.
He built his sanctuary:
      high as the heavens,
         like the earth that he established forever.

Then-
   he chose his servant David,
      whom he took from the sheepfold.
   he brought him from birthing sheep to care for Jacob,
      his people,
         Israel,
            his possession.
David shepherded them with a devoted heart,
He led them with skillful hands.

Psalm 79

A Psalm of Asaph

God Delivers Israel from Her Enemies

O God!
Heathen nations have invaded your land:
> to desecrate your holy temple,
> to destroy Jerusalem,
> to give the corpses of your servants as food for the birds of the skies;
> to give the flesh of your godly ones to the beasts of the earth;
> to make their blood flow like water around Jerusalem, with no one being buried.

We have become a reproach to our neighbors;
We have become a mockery and a derision to those around us.

O YHWH!
How long will you be angry?
Forever?
How long will your jealousy burn like fire?

Pour out your wrath upon the heathen nations that do not acknowledge you,
Pour out your wrath over the kingdoms that do not call on your name.
For:
> they consumed Jacob,
> they have made his dwelling place desolate.

Do not hold us guilty for previous iniquity,
Let your compassion come quickly to us,
> for we have been brought very low.

Help us!
O God!
Our Deliverer!

Because of your glorious name,
Deliver us!
Forgive our sins,
    because of your name.
Why should the heathen nations say, "Where is their God?"

Let divine vengeance for the blood of your servants be meted out before our eyes
    and among the heathen nations.
Let the cries of the prisoners reach you.

  With the strength of your sovereign power:
  Release those condemned to death.
  Pay back our neighbors seven times
    For the reproach with which they reproached you,
  O sovereign Lord!

Then we,
    your people,
    the sheep of your pasture,
    will praise you always.

From generation to generation,
    we will declare your praise.

Psalm 80

For the Choir Director of Music: According to the tune "The Lilies" A testimony of Asaph.

A Prayer for God to Manifest His Power

O Shepherd of Israel!
listen!

The One who leads Joseph like a flock,
The One enthroned on the cherubim,
Publically display your glory!

Manifest your sovereign power before Ephraim, Benjamin, and Manasseh,
    then come to our rescue.

O God!
Restore us!
Show your favor!
Deliver us!

O YHWH, God of the Heavenly Armies!
When will your anger toward your people's prayers cease?

You fed them tears as their food,
You caused them to drink a full measure of tears.
You have set us at strife against our neighbors,
    our enemies deride us.
O God of the Heavenly Armies!
Restore us!
Show your favor,
    so we may be delivered.

You uprooted a vine from Egypt,
   and drove out heathen nations to transplant it.
You cleared the ground so that its roots grew
   and filled the land.

Mountains were covered by its shadows,
The mighty cedars were covered by its branches.
   Its branches spread out to the Mediterranean Sea.
   Its shoots to the Euphrates River.

   Why would you break down its walls
      so that those who pass by can pluck its fruits?
   Why do wild boars of the forest gnaw at it,
      and creatures of the field feed on it?

   God of the Heavenly Armies!
   Return!
   Look down from heaven!
   See!
   Show you care for this vine.

   The root that your right hand planted,
   The shoot that you tended for yourself,
      was burned with fire, cut off,
        was destroyed on account of your rebuke.

   May you support the man at your right hand;
      the son of man whom you have raised for yourself.
   Then we will not turn away from you.

   Restore us!
   So we can call upon your name.
   God of heavenly armies!
   Restore to us the light of your favor.
   Then we will be delivered.

Experiencing God in the Psalms

Psalm 81

For the Choir Director: On the Gittith. A song by Asaph

Celebrating God's Mighty Deeds

Sing joyfully to God!
  He is our Strength.
Raise a shout to the God of Jacob!

Sing a song!
Play the tambourine,
Play the pleasant-sounding lyre along with the harp.
Blow the ram's horn when there is a new moon,
  when there is a full moon,
  on our festival day,
  because it is:
    a statute in Israel,
    an ordinance by the God of Jacob,
    a decree that he prescribed for Joseph when he went
      throughout the land of Egypt, speaking a
      language I did not recognize.

"I removed the burden from your shoulder;
  your hands were freed of the burdensome basket.
In a time of need you called out,
  I delivered you;
  I answered you from the dark thundercloud;
  I tested you at the waters of Meribah."

Musical *Interlude*

Listen!
O my people!
O Israel!

If only you would obey me!
You must neither have a foreign god over you or worship a strange god.
I am YHWH your God,
    who brought you out of the land of Egypt,
Open your mouth that I may fill it.

Yet-
    my people did not obey my voice;
    Israel did not submit to me.

So-
    I let them to continue in their stubbornness,
    living by their own advice.

If only my people would obey me,
if only Israel would walk in my ways!
Then-
    I would quickly subdue their enemies.
    I would turn against their foes.
Those who hate YHWH will cringe before him;
their punishment will be permanent.

But I will feed Israel with the finest wheat,
satisfying you with honey from the rock.

Psalm 82

A Psalm of Asaph

God Warns Human Judges

> God takes his stand in the divine assembly;
>   among the judges he renders judgment:

> "How long will you judge partially
>   by showing favor on the wicked?

Musical *Interlude*

> "Defend the poor!
>   Defend the fatherless!
>   Vindicate the afflicted!
>   Vindicate the poor!
>   Rescue the poor!
>   Rescue the needy!
>   Deliver them from the power of the wicked."

They neither know nor understand;
They walk about in the dark while all the foundations of the earth are shaken.
Indeed I said,
  "You are 'gods!'
    All of you are 'sons of the Most High.'
  But-
    like anyone else,
    you will eventually die,

    like other rulers,
    you will eventually fall."

Arise!
O God!
Judge the earth,
 for all nations belong to you.

Psalm 83

A song. A Psalm of Asaph

May God Arise and Judge the Wicked!

O God!
Do not rest!
Do not remain silent!
Do not remain inactive!

O God!
Look!
Your enemies rage;
Those who hate you:
   issue threats.
   plot against your people
   conspire against your cherished ones.

They say,
     "Let us go and erase them as a nation
     so the name of Israel
     will not be remembered anymore."

Indeed-
    they shrewdly planned together,
    they form an alliance against you—
       the clans of Edom, the Ishmaelites,
       Moab, the Hagarites, Gebal, Ammon,
       Amalek, Philistia, and the inhabitants of Tyre.
       Even Assyria joined them to strengthen the
       descendants of Lot.

Musical *Interlude*

Deal with them as you did to Midian, Sisera, and Jabin at the Kishon Brook.
They were destroyed at En-Dor and became a pile of dung on the ground.
Punish their nobles like Oreb and Zeeb.
Punish all their princes like Zebah and Zalmunna.
Punish all who said,
   "Let us possess the pastures of God."

O God!
 View and treat them:
    Like dried thistles,
    Like straw before the wind.
    Like a fire burning a forest,
    Like a flame setting mountains ablaze.

Pursue them with your storm.
Terrify them with your whirlwind.
Fill their faces with shame
   until they seek your name.

O God!
Let them be humiliated.
 Let them be terrified permanently until they die in shame.
Then they will know that you alone—
    whose name is YHWH—
are the Most High over all the earth.

Psalm 84

To the Choir Director: On the Gittith.
A Psalm by the sons of Korah.

True Happiness is in the presence of God

    How lovely are your dwelling places,
        O YHWH of the Heavenly Armies!
    I desire and long
        for the temple courts of YHWH.
    My heart and body sing for joy to the living God.

    Even-
    the sparrow found a house for herself;
    the swallow found a nest to lay her young at your altar,
    O YHWH of the Heavenly Armies!

    My king and God!
    How happy are those who live in your temple,
        for they can praise you continuously.

Musical Interlude

    How happy are those whose strength is in you,
        whose heart is on your path.
    They will pass through the Baca Valley
        where he will prepare a spring for them;
            even the early rain will cover it with blessings.
    They will walk from strength to strength;
        each will appear before God in Zion.

    O YHWH God of the Heavenly Armies!
    Hear my prayer!
    Listen!
    O God of Jacob!

Musical Interlude

O God!
Look at our shield,
Show favor to your anointed.
A day in your temple courts is better than a thousand elsewhere;
I would rather be a doorkeeper in God's house than dwell in the tent of the wicked.
    For-
        YHWH God is a sun and shield;
        YHWH grants grace and favor;
        YHWH will not withhold any good thing from those who walk blamelessly.

        O YHWH of Heavenly Armies!
        How happy are those who trust in you.

Psalm 85

To the Choir Director: A Psalm by the sons of Korah.

O YHWH,
    You have favored your land,
    You have restored the fortunes of Jacob.
    You took away the iniquity of your people,
    You forgave all their sins.

Musical *Interlude*

You withdrew all your wrath,
You turned away from your burning anger.

Restore us!
O God of our salvation!

Stop being angry with us.
Will you be angry with us forever?
Will you prolong your anger from generation to generation?
Will you restore our lives again so that your people may rejoice in you?

O YHWH!
Show us your gracious love!
Deliver us!

Let me listen to what the God YHWH says;
YHWH will promise peace to his people, to his holy ones;
May they not return to foolishness.

Surely—
    he will soon deliver those who fear him,
        for his glory will live in our land.

Gracious love and truth meet;
    righteousness and peace kiss.
Truth sprouts up from the ground,
    while righteousness looks down from the sky.
YHWH will also provide what is good,
    and our land will yield its produce.
Righteousness will go before him
    to prepare a path for his steps.

Psalm 86

A Prayer of King David

O YHWH!
Listen to me!
Answer me!

For-
    I am afflicted
    I am needy.

Protect me,
    for I am faithful.

My God!!
Deliver your servant who trusts in you.

Have mercy on me!
O sovereign Lord!
For I call on you all day long.

Your servant rejoices,
Because-
O sovereign Lord,
I set my hope on you.
Indeed-
You,
O sovereign Lord,
are:
    Kind,
    Forgiving,
    Overflowing with gracious love to everyone who calls on you.

Hear my prayer!
O YHWH!
Pay attention to my prayer of supplication!

In my troubled times I will call on you,
    for you will answer me.

No one can compare with you among the gods,
O sovereign Lord!
No one can accomplish your work.
All the nations that you have established will come and worship you,
My sovereign Lord.

They will honor your name.
For-
    you are great,
    you are doing awesome things;
    you alone are God.

Teach me your ways
O YHWH!
So that:
    I may walk in your truth;
    I may wholeheartedly fear your name.

I will praise you,
O sovereign Lord my God.
With my whole being,
I will honor your name continuously.

Great is your gracious love to me;
You have delivered me from the depths of the afterlife.
O God!
Arrogant men rise up against me,
A company of ruthless individuals want to kill me.

They do not have regard for you.

But-
You,
O sovereign Lord,
Are:
    a compassionate God,
    a merciful God,
    a patient God,
    a God of unending gracious love and faithfulness.

Return to me!
Have mercy on me!
Clothe your servant with your strength!
Deliver the son of your maid servant!

Show me a sign of your goodness,
    so that those who hate me will see it and be ashamed.

For-
You,
O sovereign Lord!
    will help me,
    will comfort me.

Psalm 87

A Psalm by the sons of Korah. A song.

> God's sovereign throne is established in the holy mountains.
> YHWH loves the gates of Zion more than the dwellings of Jacob.
>
> Glorious things are spoken of you,
> O city of God!

Musical Interlude

> I will mention Rahab and Babylon among those who acknowledge me including
> Philistia, Tyre, and Ethiopia.
>
> They say-
>> "This one was born there."
>
> Indeed-
> about Zion it will be said:
>> "More than one person was born in it,"
>> "The Most High himself did it."
>
> YHWH will record,
>> as he registers the peoples,
>>> "This one was born there."

Musical *Interlude*

> Then singers,
>> as they play their instruments,
> will declare,
>> "All my foundations are in you."

Psalm 88

A song. A Psalm by the sons of Korah. According to the tune Mahalat Leannoth. A maskil by Heman the Ezrahite.

A Cry to YHWH for Help

   O YHWH!
   O God of my salvation!

   I cry out to you day and night!
   Let my prayer come before you!
   Listen to my cry!
   For my life is filled with troubles as I approach the afterlife.

   I am considered:
      Like those descending into the afterlife,
      Like a mighty man without strength,
      Like a mighty man released to remain with the dead,
         lying in a grave like a corpse,
         remembered no longer,
         cut off from your power.

   You have assigned me:
         to the lowest part of the pit,
         to the darkest depths.

   Your anger lays heavily upon me;
   You pound me with all your waves.

Musical *Interlude*

   You caused my acquaintances to shun me;
   You make me extremely abhorrent to them.
   I am restrained,
   I am unable to go out.

My eyes languish on account of my affliction;
All day long I call out to you,
O YHWH!

I spread out my hands up to you.

Can you publicly perform wonders for the dead?
Can departed spirits stand up publicly to praise you?

Musical Interlude

Can your gracious love be publicly declared in the afterlife?
Can your faithfulness be publicly declared in Abaddon?
Can your awesome deeds be publicly known in darkness
Can your righteousness be publicly known in the land of oblivion?

As for me,
I cry out to you YHWH,
In the morning my prayer greets you.

O YHWH!
Why have you rejected me?
Why have you hidden your face from me?

Since my youth:
    I have been oppressed,
    I have been in danger of death.
    I bear your dread,
    I am overwhelmed.

Your burning anger overwhelms me;
Your terrors destroy me.
    They engulf me all day long like flood waters;
    They surround me on all sides.

You caused my friend and neighbor to shun me;
You caused my acquaintances to be confused.

Psalm 89

A Maskil. By Ethan, the Ezrahite
YHWH's Covenant with David

    I will publicly sing forever about the gracious love of YHWH;
        from generation to generation
    I will publicly declare your faithfulness with my mouth.
    I will publicly declare that your gracious love was established forever;

    In the heavens itself-
        you have established your faithfulness.

    "I have made a covenant with my chosen one;
    I have made a promise to David, my servant.
        'I will establish your dynasty forever,
            I will lift up one who will build your throne
                from generation to generation.'"

Musical *Interlude*

    Even the heavens praise your awesome deeds,
    O YHWH!
    Even your faithfulness in the assembly of the holy ones.

    Who in the heavens can compare to YHWH?
    Who is like YHWH among the gods?
    God is:
        feared in the council of the holy ones,
        feared by all those around him.

    O YHWH!
    God of the Heavenly Armies!
    Who is as mighty as you?

O YHWH!
Your faithfulness surrounds you.

You rule over the majestic sea;
    when its waves surge,
      you calm them.
You crushed Rahab (i.e. Egypt) to death;
With your powerful arm you scattered your enemies.

Heaven and the earth belong to you,
   the world and everything it contains—
you established them.
   The north and south—
you created them;
    Tabor and Hermon joyously praise your name.

Your arm is strong;
Your hand is mighty;
Indeed-
your right hand is victorious.
Righteousness and justice make up the foundation of your throne;
Gracious love and truth meet before you.

How happy are the people who can worship you joyfully!
O YHWH!
They walk in the light of your presence.

In your name:
    they rejoice all day long,
    they exult in your justice.

For you are their strength's grandeur;
by your favor you exalted our power.

Indeed-
>   our shield belongs to YHWH,
>   our king to the Holy One of Israel.

You spoke to your faithful ones through a vision:
>   "I will set a young man over a warrior.
>   I will raise up a chosen one from the people.
>   I have found my servant David;
>   I have anointed him with my sacred oil,
>   with whom my power will be firmly established;
>   for my arm will strengthen him.
>   No enemy will deceive him;
>   No wicked person will afflict him.
>   I will crush his enemies before him
>   I will strike those who hate him.
>   My faithfulness and gracious love will be with him,
>   In my name his power will be exalted.
>   I will place his hand over the sea,
>   His right hand over the rivers."

He will announce to me
>   "You are my father,
>   My God,
>   the Rock of my salvation."

Indeed-
>   "I myself made him the first born,
>   the highest of the kings of the earth.
>   I will show my gracious love toward him forever,
>   since my covenant is securely established with him.
>   I will establish his dynasty forever,
>   and his throne as long as heaven endures.

But-
>if his sons:
>>abandon my laws
>>do not follow my ordinances,
>>profane my statutes;
>>do not keep my commands.

Then-
>I will punish their disobedience with a rod
>I will punish their iniquity with lashes.

But-
>I will not cut off my gracious love from him,
>I will not stop being faithful.
>I will not dishonor my covenant,
>I will not change what I have spoken.

>I have sworn by my holiness once for all:
>I will not lie to David.
>>His dynasty will last forever
>>His throne will be like the sun before me.
>>His throne will be established forever like the moon,
>>>a faithful witness in the sky."

Musical Interlude

>But-
>You have spurned, rejected, and become angry with your anointed;
>You have dishonored the covenant with your servant;
>You have defiled his crown on the ground.
>You have broken through all his walls;
>You have laid his fortresses in ruin.

All who pass by on their way plunder him;
  He has become a reproach to his neighbors.

You have exalted the right hand of his adversaries;
You have caused all of his enemies to rejoice.
Moreover-

You have turned back the edge of his sword,
You did not support him in battle.
You have caused his splendor to cease
You cast down his throne to the ground.
You have caused the days of his youth to be cut short;
You have covered him with shame."

Musical Interlude

  How long?
  O YHWH!
  Will you hide yourself forever?
  Will your anger continuously burn like fire?
  Remember-
  How short my lifetime is!
  How powerless have you created all human beings!
  What valiant man can live and not see death
  Who can deliver himself from the power of the afterlife?

Musical Interlude

  Where is your gracious love of old,
  O sovereign Lord?
  That in your faithfulness you promised to David?
  Remember-
    O sovereign Lord!
  the reproach of your servant!

I carry inside me all the insults of many people,
   when your enemies reproached you,
O YHWH!
   they reproached the footsteps of your anointed.

Blessed is YHWH forever!
   Amen and amen!

BOOK IV (PSALMS 90-106)

This Scroll gathers together wonderful stories of YHWH's mighty sovereign deeds in the past, beginning with Moses and the Exodus. This inspires us to trust that He will deliver us in our own day. YHWH's absolute sovereignty over all things is celebrated as the foundation of our only hope in this life and in the next.

Psalm 90

A prayer by Moses

YHWH is Our Refuge

O sovereign Lord!
You have been our refuge from generation to generation.

Before the mountains were formed,
Before the earth and the world were brought forth,
You are God from eternity to eternity!

You return people to dust by merely saying,
   "Return to dust,
      you mortals!"

One thousand years in your sight are but a single day that passes by,
   just like a night watch.
You will sweep them away while they are asleep.

By morning, they are like growing grass.
In the morning, the grass blossoms and is renewed,
But toward evening, the grass fades and withers away.

Indeed-
   we are consumed by your anger;
   we are terrified by your wrath.
You have set our iniquities before you,
   what we have concealed from the light of your presence.

All our days pass away in your wrath;
Our years fade away and end like a sigh.

We live for 70 or 80 years, if we are healthy.

Yet-
    even in the prime years;
    there are troubles and sorrow,
    they pass by quickly,
    then we fly away.

Who can know the intensity of your anger?
    Because our fear of you matches your wrath,
Teach us to keep watch over our days,
    so we may develop inner wisdom.

Please return to us!
O YHWH!
When will it be?

Comfort your servants.
Satisfy us in the morning with your gracious love
So:
    we may sing for joy
    we may rejoice every day.
Cause us to rejoice throughout the time when you have afflicted us,
    the years when we have known trouble.

May your awesome deeds be revealed to your servants,
    as well as your splendor to their children.

May your favor rain upon us!
O YHWH our God!

Make our endeavors successful!
Yes-
Make our endeavors secure!

Psalm 91

A Psalm of David

God is Our Only Refuge

> The one who lives in the shelter of the Most High,
> The one who rests in the shadow of the Almighty,
>> will say to YHWH,
>>> "You are
>>>> my refuge,
>>>> my fortress,
>>>> my God
>>>> in whom I trust!"
>
> He will surely deliver you from the hunter's snare;
> He will surely deliver you from the destructive plague.
> With his feathers he will cover you,
>> under his wings you will find safety.
> His truth is your shield and armor.
>
> You need not fear:
>> the terror that stalks in the night,
>> the arrow that flies in the day,
>> the plague that strikes in the darkness,
>> the calamity that destroys at noon.
>
> If a thousand fell at your side;
> If ten thousand fell at your right hand,
>> it will not overcome you.
> Only observe it with your eyes,
> You will see how the wicked are paid back.

"O YHWH!
 You are my refuge!"

 Because you chose the Most High as your dwelling place,
     no evil will fall upon you,
     no affliction will approach your tent,
 for he will command his angels to protect you in all your ways.
 With their hands they will lift you up so you will not be dashed
 on a stone.

 You will crush lions and snakes;
 You will trample young lions and serpents.

 Because he has focused his love on me,
     "I will deliver him.
      I will protect him."
 Because he knows my name.
 When he calls out to me,
     "I will answer him.
      I will be with him in his distress.
      I will deliver him,
      I will honor him.
      I will satisfy him with long life;
      I will show him my deliverance."

Psalm 92

A Psalm for the Sabbath Day

Give Thanks to YHWH

It is good to give thanks to YHWH!
It is good to sing praise to your name,
O Most High!

It is good to proclaim:
    your gracious love in the morning;
    your faithfulness at night,
        accompanied by a ten-stringed instrument and a lyre,
        accompanied by the contemplative sound of a harp.

Because you made me glad with your awesome deeds,
O YHWH!
I will sing for joy at the works of your hands.

How great are your works,
O YHWH!

Your thoughts are unfathomable.

A stupid man does not know,
A fool cannot comprehend this:
  Though the wicked sprout like grass;
  And all who practice iniquity flourish,
     it is they who will be eternally devastated.
But you are exalted forever,
O YHWH!
Look at your enemies!
O YHWH!

Look at your enemies,

for they are destroyed;

Everyone who practices iniquity will be scattered.

You have grown my strength like the horn of a wild ox;
I was anointed with fresh oil.
My eyes gloated over those who lie in wait for me;
    when those of evil intent attack me,
        my ears will hear.

The righteous will flourish like palm trees;
They will grow like a cedar in Lebanon.

Planted in YHWH's temple:
    They will flourish in the courtyard of our God.
    They will still bear fruit even in old age;
    They will be luxuriant and green.
    They will proclaim:
        "YHWH is upright, my Rock,
            in whom there is no injustice."

Psalm 93

YHWH is Sovereign Over All Things

YHWH reigns!

YHWH is:
    clothed in majesty,
    clothed in sovereignty,
    girded with strength.

Indeed-
    the world is well established,
    the world cannot be shaken.

Your throne has been established since time immemorial;
You are king from eternity!

O YHWH!
The rivers:
    have flooded,
    have spoken aloud,
    have lifted up their crushing waves.

More than the sound of surging waters
    (the majestic waves of the sea)
YHWH on high is majestic.

Your decrees are very trustworthy,
Your holiness always befits your house,
O YHWH!

Psalm 94

YHWH Is a God of Vengeance

O God of vengeance!
O YHWH God of vengeance!

Demonstrate your splendor!
Stand up!
O Judge of the earth,
Repay the proud.

How long will the wicked,
O YHWH!
How long will the wicked continue to triumph?

When they speak,
    they are arrogant.
Everyone who practices iniquity brags about it.

O YHWH!
They have crushed your people,
They have afflicted your heritage.
The wicked kill widows and foreigners;
They murder orphans.
They say,
    "YHWH cannot see,
      the God of Jacob will not notice."
Pay attention!
O you stupid ones among the people!
You fools!
Will you ever become wise?
The One:
    who formed the ear can hear, can he not?
    who made the eyes can see, can he not?

who disciplines nations can rebuke them, can he not?
who teaches mankind can discern, can he not?

YHWH knows that the thoughts of human beings are futile.

How blessed is the man whom you instruct,
O YHWH!
The one whom you teach from your Torah
   keeping him calm when times are troubled,
      until a pit has been dug for the wicked.

YHWH:
   will not forsake his people;
      will not abandon his heritage.

Righteousness will be restored with justice,
All the pure of heart will follow it.

Who will rise up for me against the wicked?
Who will stand for me against those who practice iniquity?
If YHWH had not been my helper,
I would have quickly become silent.

O YHWH!
When I say that my foot is shaking,
Your gracious love will sustain me.

When my anxious thoughts overwhelm me,
your comfort encourages me.

Will destructive politicians—
   who plan wicked things through their misuse of the
      Torah—
be allied with you?
They gather together against the righteous,
They condemn the innocent to death.

But-
YHWH is:
>   my Stronghold,
>   my God,
>   my Rock,
>   my Refuge.

He will:
>   repay them for their sin;
>   destroy them because of their evil.

YHWH our God will devastate them!

Psalm 95

Sing Joyfully to YHWH

O come!
Let us sing joyfully to YHWH!
Let us shout for joy to the rock of our salvation.
Let us come into his presence with thanksgiving;
Let us shout with songs of praise to him.

For YHWH is an awesome God;
    a great king above all heavenly beings.
He holds in his hand the lowest parts of the earth
    and the mountain peaks belong to him.
The sea that he made belongs to him,
    along with the dry land that his hands formed.

O come!
Let us:
    worship and bow down;
    kneel before YHWH who made us.
For he is our God:
    we are the people of his pasture
    we are the flock in his care.
If only:
    you would listen to his voice today,
    do not be stubborn like your ancestors were Meribah,
    as on that day at Massah, in the wilderness, when your ancestors tested me.
They tested me,
    even though they had seen my awesome deeds.

For forty years I loathed that generation, so I said,
    "They are a people whose hearts continually err,
    They have not understood my ways."

So, in my anger, I declared an oath:
   "They shall not enter my rest."

Psalm 96

Give Glory to YHWH

>Sing to YHWH!
>>All the earth!
>
>Sing to YHWH!
>>Bless his name!
>>Proclaim his deliverance every day!
>>Declare his glory among the nations
>>Declare his awesome deeds among all the peoples!
>
>YHWH is great,
>>and greatly to be praised;
>
>He is awesome above all gods.
>>For all the gods of the peoples are worthless idols,
>
>But-
>>YHWH made the heavens.
>>Splendor and majesty are before him;
>>might and beauty are in his sanctuary.
>
>Ascribe to YHWH, you families of peoples,
>Ascribe to YHWH glory and strength!
>Ascribe to YHWH the glory due his name,
>
>Bring an offering and enter his courts!
>Worship YHWH in holy splendor;
>Tremble before him, all the earth.

Declare among the nations,
> "YHWH reigns!
> Indeed, he established the world so that it will
> not falter. He will judge people with justice."

The heavens will be glad
The earth will rejoice-
> even the sea and everything that fills it will roar-

The field and all that is in it will rejoice;
Then all the trees of the forest will sing for joy before YHWH,
> because he is coming;

Indeed-
> he will come to judge the earth.

He will judge the world in justice;
He will judge its people with justice.

Psalm 97

YHWH is Sovereign Over All Things

>YHWH reigns in sovereignty!
>>Let the earth rejoice!
>>May many islands be glad!

Thick clouds are all around him;
Righteousness and justice are his throne's foundation.
Fire goes out from his presence to consume his enemies on every side.
His lightning bolts light the world;
  The earth sees and shakes.
Mountains melt like wax before YHWH—
  before YHWH of all the earth.

The heavens declare his righteousness
    so that all the nations see his glory.

All who serve carved images;
All those who praise idols;
   will be humiliated.

Worship him,
   all you so-called "gods"!

Zion hears and rejoices;
The towns of Judah rejoice on account of your justice,
O YHWH!

O YHWH!
For:
    you are the Most High above all the earth;
    you are exalted high above all heavenly beings.

Hate evil!
You who love YHWH!

He guards the lives of those who love him,
    delivering them from domination by the wicked.
Light shines on the righteous;
    gladness on the morally upright.
Rejoice in YHWH,
    you righteous ones!
Give thanks at the mention of his holiness!

Psalm 98

A Psalm

Sing Praises to the Sovereign King

>Sing to YHWH a new song,
>>for he has done awesome deeds!
>
>His right hand and powerful arm
>>have brought him the victory.
>
>YHWH:
>>has made his deliverance known;
>>has disclosed his justice before the nations.
>>has remembered his gracious love;
>>his faithfulness toward the house of Israel;
>
>All the ends of the earth saw our God's deliverance.
>
>Make a joyful noise to YHWH,
>all the earth!
>Break forth into joyful songs of praise!
>Sing praises to YHWH:
>>with a lyre;
>>>(with a lyre and a melodious song)
>>>with trumpets;
>>>with the sound of a ram's horn.
>
>Shout in the presence of YHWH, the Sovereign King!
>
>Let the sea and everything in it shout,
>>along with the world and its inhabitants;
>
>Let the rivers clap their hands in unison;
>Let the mountains sing for joy before YHWH,
>>who comes to judge the earth;
>
>He will judge the world righteously;
>He will judge its people with justice.

Psalm 99

YHWH is Holy

> YHWH reigns in sovereignty!
>> let the people tremble;
>
> He is seated above the cherubim—
>> let the earth quake.
>
> YHWH is great in Zion
>> and is exalted above all peoples.
>
> Let them praise your great and awesome name.
>> He is holy!
>
> A mighty king who loves justice,
>> you have established fairness.
>> you have exercised justice and righteousness over Jacob.
>
> Exalt YHWH our God!
> Worship him!
> Bow down at his footstool!
> He is holy!
>
> Moses and Aaron were among his priests;
> Samuel also was among those who invoked his name.
> When they called on YHWH,
>> he answered them.
>
> In a pillar of cloud,
>> he spoke to them.
>
> They obeyed his decrees;
> He gave them the Torah.

YHWH our God!
    You answered them;
    You were their God who forgave them;
    You also avenged their evil deeds.

Exalt YHWH our God!
Worship at his holy mountain!
    For YHWH our God is holy!

Psalm 100

A Psalm of Thanksgiving to YHWH

Shout to YHWH all the earth!

Serve YHWH with joy.
Come before him with a joyful singing!

Acknowledge that YHWH, He is God.
He made us and we belong to him;

We are his people;
We are the sheep of his pasture.

Enter his gates with thanksgiving
Enter his courts with praise.

Thank him and bless his name,
   For YHWH is good.

His gracious love stands forever.
His faithfulness remains from generation to generation.

Psalm 101

A Psalm of David
YHWH's Grace and Love

    I will sing of YHWH's gracious love and justice.

O YHWH!
I will sing praise to you.
I will pay attention to living a life of justice—
    (When will I attain it?)
I will live with integrity of heart in my house.
I will not even think about doing anything that violates the
 Torah.
I hate to do evil deeds;
I will have none of it.
I will not allow anyone with a perverted mind in my presence;
I will not be involved with anything evil.
I will destroy the one who secretly slanders a friend.
I will not allow the proud and haughty to prevail.

    My eyes are looking at the faithful of the land,
        so they may live with me;

    The one who lives a life of justice will serve me.
        A deceitful person will not sit in my house;
        A liar will not remain in my presence.
Every morning I will destroy all the wicked of the land,
Eliminating everyone who practices iniquity from YHWH's city.

Psalm 102

A prayer to YHWH for Help

O YHWH!
    Hear my prayer!
    May my cry for help come to you.
    Do not hide your face from me when I am in trouble.
    Listen to me!

When I call to out you,
    hurry to answer me!
For:
    my days are vanishing like smoke;
    my bones are charred as in a fireplace.

Withered like grass, my heart is overwhelmed,
I have even forgotten to eat my food.
Because of the sound of my sighing,
    my bones cling to my skin.
    I resemble a pelican in the wilderness,
    an owl in a desolate land.

I lie awake,
Yet-
    I am like a bird isolated on a rooftop.

My enemies:
    revile me all day long;
    ridicule me;
    use my name to curse.

I have eaten ashes as food
I have mixed my drink with tears.
Because of your indignation and wrath,
    When:

you lifted me,
you cast me away.
My life is like a declining shadow,
I am withering like a plant.

O YHWH!
You are enthroned forever;
You are remembered throughout all generations.
You will arise to extend compassion on Zion,
    for it is time to show her favor—
        the appointed time has come.
Your servants take pleasure in its stones
        and delight in its debris.

Nations will fear the name of YHWH,
All the kings of the earth will fear your splendor.

When YHWH rebuilds Zion,
    he will appear in his glory.
    he will turn to the prayer of the destitute,
        not despising their prayer.
Write this for the next generation,
    that a people yet to be created will praise YHWH.
When he looked down from his holy heights—
    YHWH looked over the earth from heaven—
        to listen to the groans of prisoners,
        to set free those condemned to death,
            so-
        they would declare the name of YHWH in Zion
        they would declare his praise in Jerusalem,
            when people and kingdoms gather together to
            serve YHWH.

He has weakened my strength along the way.
He has cut short my days.

I say,
> "My God, whose years continue through all generations,
> do not take me in the middle of my life."

You established the earth long ago;
The heavens are the work of your hands.
They will perish,
But- you will remain;
They all will become worn out like a garment.
You will change them like clothing,
    and they will pass away.
But you remain the same;
    your years never end.
May the descendants of your servants live securely,
May their children be established in your presence.

Psalm 103

A Psalm of David

Bless YHWH for All Things

> Bless YHWH!
> O my soul!
>
> All that is within me,
> bless his holy name.
>
> Bless YHWH!
> O my soul!
>
> Do not forget any of his benefits:
> > He continues to forgive all your sins,
> > He continues to heal all your diseases,
> > He continues to redeem your life from the pit,
> > He continually surrounds you with love and compassion.
> > He keeps satisfying you with good things,
> > He keeps renewing your youth like the eagles.
>
> YHWH continually does what is right,
> > He executes justice for all who are being oppressed.
> > He revealed his will to Moses,
> > He revealed his deeds to the people of Israel.
> YHWH is:
> > Compassionate,
> > Gracious,
> > Patient,
> > Abundantly rich in gracious love.
>
> He does not chasten continuously;
> He does not remain distant forever.

He does not deal with us according to our sins,
He does not repay us for our iniquity.

As high as the heavens are above earth,
   so his gracious love surrounds those who fear him.
As distant as the east is from the west,
   that is how far he has removed our sins from us.

As a father has compassion for his children,
   Even so YHWH has compassion for those who fear him.

He knows how we were created,
He knows that we were made from dirt.

A man's life is like grass—
   it blossoms like wild flowers,
   when the wind blows on it, it withers away,
   no one remembers that it ever existed.
Yet-
   YHWH's gracious love remains throughout eternity for those who fear him;
   His righteous acts extend to their children's children,
      to those who keep his covenant,
      to those who remember to observe his precepts.

YHWH has established his sovereign throne in the heavens;
His sovereignty rules over all things.

Bless YHWH!
   You angels who belong to him,
   You mighty warriors who carry out his commands,
   You who are obedient to the sound of his words.

Bless YHWH!
   all his heavenly armies,
   his ministers who do his will.

Bless YHWH!
   all his creation,
      in all the places of his dominion.

Bless YHWH!
   O my soul!

Psalm 104

A Psalm of David

Praise YHWH, The Creator and Sustainer of all Things

  Bless YHWH!
  O my soul!

  O YHWH!
  My God:
      You are very great.
      You are clothed in splendor and majesty;
      You are wrapped in light like a garment,
      stretching out the sky like a curtain.

  He lays the beams of his roof on the waters above,
     making clouds his chariot,
        walking on the wings of the wind.
  He makes the winds his messengers,
  He makes blazing fires his servants.
  He established the earth on its foundations,
     so that it never falters.

  You cover the seas like a garment;
     the water stood above the mountains.
  They flee at your rebuke;
  They fly away at the sound of your thunders.
  Mountains rise up and valleys sink to the place you have ordained for them.
  You have set a boundary they cannot cross;
  They will never again cover the earth.

He causes springs to gush forth into rivers that flow between the mountains.
They give water for animals of the field to drink;
   the wild donkeys quench their thirst.

Birds of the sky live beside them;
  They sing a song among the foliage.

He waters the mountains from the heavens;
The earth is satisfied from the fruit of your work.
He causes grass to sprout for the cattle;
He makes plants for people to cultivate to produce food from the land,
     wine that makes the heart of people happy,
     olive oil that makes the face glow,
     food that sustains people.

The loftiest trees are satisfied,
Even the cedars of Lebanon that he planted,
   the birds build their nests there,
   the heron builds its nest among the evergreen.
The high mountains are for wild goats;
   the cliffs are a refuge for the rock badger.

He made the moon to mark time;
   the sun knows its setting time.
You bring darkness and it becomes night;
   when every beast of the forest prowls.
Young lions roar for prey,
   seeking their food from God.
When the sun rises, they gather
   and lie down in their dens.
People go out to their work
   and labor until evening.

How numerous are your works,
O YHWH!
You have made them all wisely;
The earth is filled with your creations.

There is the deep and wide sea,
    teeming with numberless creatures,
        living things small and great.
There-
    the ships pass through;
    Leviathan- which you created- frolics in it.

All of them look up to you to provide them their food at the proper time.
They receive what you give them.

When you open your hand-
    they are filled with good things.
When you withdraw your favor,
    they are disappointed.
Take away their breath,
they die,
they return to dust.

When you send your Spirit,
they are created.
Thus you replenish the surface of the earth.

May the glory of YHWH last forever;
May YHWH rejoice in his works!

He looks at the earth and it shakes;
He touches the mountains and they smoke.

I will sing to YHWH with my whole being;
I will sing to my God continuously!

May my thoughts be pleasing to him;
Indeed-
I will rejoice in YHWH!

May sinners disappear from the land,
May the wicked live no longer.

Bless YHWH!
  O my soul!

Hallelujah!

Psalm 105

Thanksgiving for God's Deliverance

Give thanks to YHWH,
Call on his name,
Make his deeds known among the people.

Sing to him!
Praise him!
Declare all his awesome deeds!
Exult in his holy name!
Let all those who seek YHWH rejoice!

Seek YHWH and his strength;
Seek his face continuously.

Remember his awesome deeds that he has done,
Remember his wonders and the judgments he declared.

You descendants of Abraham, his servant,
You children of Jacob, his chosen ones.
    "He is YHWH our God!
    His judgments extend to the entire earth.
    He remembers his eternal covenant—
      He remembers every promise he made for a thousand generations,
        like the covenant he made with Abraham,
        like his promise to Isaac."
He presented it to Jacob as a decree,
He presented it to Israel as an everlasting covenant.

He said:
> "I will give Canaan to you as the allotted portion that is your inheritance."

When the Hebrews were few in number—so very few—
When they were sojourners in it,
> they wandered from nation to nation,
> they wandered from one kingdom to another.

He did not allow anyone to oppress them,
He did not allow any kings to reprove them.
> "Do not touch my anointed
> or hurt my prophets!"

He declared a famine on the land;
> destroying the entire food supply.

He sent a man before them— Joseph,
> Who had been sold as a slave,
> Who bound his feet with fetters,
> Who placed an iron collar on his neck,
>> until the time his prediction came true,
>> as the word of YHWH refined him.

He sent a king who released him,
He sent a ruler of the people who set him free.
He made him the master over his household,
He made him the manager of all his possessions,
> to discipline his rulers at will,
> to make his elders wise.

Then Israel came to Egypt;
Indeed-
Jacob lived in the land of Ham.

He caused his people to multiply greatly;
He caused them to be more numerous than their enemies.
He caused their enemies to hate his people

He caused them to deceive his servants.
He sent his servant Moses, along with Aaron,
    whom he had chosen.
They performed his signs among them,
They performed his wonders in the land of Ham.

He sent darkness,
it became dark.

Did they not rebel against his words?

He turned their water into blood,
    so that the fish died.
Their land swarmed with frogs
    even to the chambers of their kings.
He spoke,
    and a swarm of insects invaded their land.

He sent hail instead of rain,
He sent lightning throughout their land.
It destroyed their vines and their figs,
    breaking trees throughout their country.

Then he commanded the locust to come—
    grasshoppers without number.
They consumed every green plant in their land,
They devoured the fruit of their soil.

He struck down every firstborn in their land,
    the first fruits of all their progeny.

Then he brought Israel out with silver and gold,
no one among his tribes stumbled.
The Egyptians rejoiced when they left,
    because fear of Israel descended on them.

He spread out a cloud for a cover during the day,
He spread out a fire for light at night.

Israel asked,
The quail came;
Food from heaven satisfied them.
 He opened a rock,
  water gushed out flowing like a river in the desert.

Indeed-
He remembered his sacred promise to his servant Abraham.
He led his people out with gladness,
He led his elect ones with shouts of joy.
He gave to them the land of nations;
They inherited the labor of other people so that:
    they might keep his statutes
     they might observe his laws.

Hallelujah!

Psalm 106

The Goodness of God and the Wickedness of Israel

Hallelujah!

Give thanks to YHWH,
Because-
   he is good,
    his grace and love exist forever.

Who can fully describe the mighty acts of YHWH?
Who can fully proclaim all his praises?

How happy are those who enforce justice,
How happy are those who live righteously all the time.

Remember me!
O YHWH!
When you show favor to your people.

Visit us with your deliverance,
   to witness the prosperity of your elect ones,
   to rejoice in your nation's joy,
   to glory in your inheritance.

We have sinned along with our ancestors;
We have committed iniquity and wickedness.
In Egypt-
   our ancestors did not comprehend your awesome deeds.
   our ancestors did not remember your abundant gracious love.
Instead-
   they rebelled beside the sea, the Red Sea.
He delivered for the sake of his name,
He delivered them to make his power known.

He shouted at the Red Sea and it dried up;
He led them through the sea as though through a desert.
He delivered them from the power of their foe;
He redeemed them from the power of their enemy.

> The water overwhelmed their enemies,
> Not one of them survived.

> Then they believed his word,
> Then they sang his praise.

> But-
> They quickly forgot his deeds
> They did not wait for his counsel.
> They were overwhelmed with craving in the wilderness.

God tested them in the desert.
God granted them their request,
God sent leanness into their souls.

They were envious of Moses in the camp,
They were envious of Aaron, the holy one of YHWH.

> The earth opened;
>> It swallowed Dathan,
>> It closed over Abiram's family.

> A fire burned among their company,
> A flame set the wicked ablaze.

They fashioned a calf at Horeb.
They worshipped a carved image.
They exchanged their Glory for the image of a grass-eating bull.
They forgot God their Savior,
> who performed great things in Egypt,

who performed awesome deeds in the land of Ham,
who performed astonishing deeds at the Red Sea.

He would have destroyed them but for Moses,
his chosen one, who stood in the breach before him to avert
his destructive wrath.

They rejected the desirable land,
They did not trust his promise.
They murmured in their tents,
They did not listen to the voice of YHWH.

So he swore an oath concerning them that—
> he would cause them to die in the wilderness,
> he would cause their children to perish among the nations
> he would cause them to be scattered among many lands.

For-
> they adopted the worship of Baal Peor;
> they ate sacrifices offered to the dead.
> they had provoked His anger by their deeds,
> so that a plague broke out against them.

But-
> Phinehas intervened and prayed,
> so that the plague was restrained.
It was credited to him as a righteous act,
> from generation to generation—to eternity.

They provoked God's wrath at the waters of Meribah,
Moses suffered on account of them.
But-
> they rebelled against him,
> so that he spoke thoughtlessly with his lips.

They never destroyed the heathen,
   as YHWH had commanded them.
Instead-
   they mingled among the heathen nations
   they learned their ways.
   they worshipped their idols,
      this became a snare for them.
   they sacrificed their sons and daughters to demons.
   they shed innocent blood—
      the blood of their sons and daughters—
      whom they sacrificed to the idols of Canaan,
      polluting the land with blood.

Therefore-
      they became unclean because of what they did;
      they have acted like whores by their evil deeds.

YHWH's anger burned against his people:
   He despised his own inheritance.
   He turned them over to domination by nations
   where those who hated them ruled over them.
Their enemies oppressed them,
   so that they were humiliated by their power.
He delivered them over to them many times.

But-
   they demonstrated rebellion by their evil plans;
   they sank deep in their sins.

Yet-
   when he saw their distress,
   when he heard their cries for help.
 He remembered his covenant with them,
 He relented according to the greatness of his gracious love.
 He caused all their captors to show compassion toward them.

Deliver us!
O YHWH our God!

Gather us from among the nations so:
    we may praise your holy name
    we may rejoice in praising you.

Blessed are you,
O YHWH God of Israel,
from eternity to eternity.

Let all the people say, "Amen!"

Hallelujah!

BOOK V (PSALMS 107-150)

This scroll gathers Pre and Post-Exilic Psalms that express the desire of God's people for personal and national deliverance. The Psalmists argue from personal deliverance, and the history of the Exodus to national deliverance.

Psalm 107

Gratitude for God's Deliverance

O give thanks to YHWH!
He is good!
His gracious love exists forever!

Let those who have been redeemed by YHWH proclaim it—
    those whom he redeemed from the power of the enemy,
    those whom he gathered from other lands,
    those whom he has gathered from the east, west, north, and south.

They wandered in desolate wilderness;
They found no road to a city where they could live.
Hungry and thirsty, their spirits failed.
Then they cried out to YHWH in their trouble:
    He delivered them from their distress.
    He led them in a straight way to find a city where they could live.

Let them give thanks to YHWH
    For:
        his gracious love,
        his awesome deeds for mankind.
        He has satisfied the one who thirsts,
        filling the hungry with what is good.

Some sat in deepest darkness,
    shackled with cruel iron,
        because:
            they rebelled against the command of God,
            they despised the advice of the Most High.

He humbled them through suffering,
   as they stumbled without a helper.

Then they cried out to YHWH in their trouble:
     he delivered them from their distress.
     he brought them out from darkness and the shadow of death,
     he shattered their chains.

Let them give thanks to YHWH:
     for his gracious love,
     for his awesome deeds to mankind,
     for he shattered bronze gates,
     for he cut through iron bars.

Because of their rebellious ways,
   fools suffered for their iniquities.
They loathed all food,
   even reaching the gates of death.

Yet:
    when they cried out to YHWH in their trouble:
     he delivered them from certain destruction.
     he issued his command and healed them;
     he delivered them from their destruction.

Let them give thanks to YHWH:
     for his gracious love,
     for his awesome deeds for mankind.

Let them offer sacrifices of thanksgiving
Let them talk about his works with shouts of joy.

Those:
    who go down to the sea in ships,
    who work in the great waters,

who witnessed the works of YHWH;
who witnessed his awesome deeds in the ocean's depth,
He spoke and it stirred up a storm that made its waves surge.

The people:
    ascended skyward,
    descended to the depths,
    their courage melting away in their peril.
    They reeled and staggered like a drunkard,
    as all their wisdom became useless.

Yet-
    when they cried out to YHWH in their trouble,
    YHWH brought them out of their distress.
    He calmed the storm,
    its waves quieted down.
    they rejoiced that the waves became quiet,
    he led them to their desired haven.

Let them give thanks to YHWH:
    for his gracious love;
    for his awesome deeds on behalf of mankind.

Let them exalt him in the assembly of the people
Let them praise him in the counsel of the elders.

He turns:
    rivers into a desert,
    springs of water into dry ground.
    a fruitful land into a salty waste,
        due to the wickedness of its inhabitants.

He also turns:
    a desert into a pool of water,
    a dry land into springs of water.

There he settled the hungry,
    where they built a city to live in.
They sowed fields and planted vineyards that yielded a productive harvest.
Then he blessed them:
    they became numerous;
    he multiplied their cattle.
But-
    they became few in number,
    Humiliated by continued oppression, agony, and sorrow.

Having poured contempt on their nobles,
He caused them to err aimlessly in the way.

Yet-
    he lifted the needy from affliction,
    he made them families like a flock.

The upright see it and rejoice.
But-
    the mouth of an evil person is shut.

Let whoever is wise observe these things,
    that they may comprehend the gracious love of YHWH.

Psalm 108

A song of David.

    My heart is fixed!
    O God!
    I will publicly sing and praise you with my whole being.

    Awake, harp and lyre!
    I will wake at dawn.
    I will give you thanks among the peoples,
    O YHWH!

    I will sing praise to you among the nations.
        For your gracious love extends to the sky,
            and your faithfulness reaches to the clouds.
    May you be exalted above the heavens.

    O God!
    May your glory be over all the earth.

    In order that those you love may be rescued,
        deliver them with your power and answer me!

    God had promised in his sanctuary:

        "I will triumph and divide Shechem,
         then I will measure the valley of Succoth!
         Gilead and Manasseh belong to me,
          while Ephraim is my chief stronghold
          and Judah is my scepter. Moab is my washbasin;
         I will fling my shoe on Edom,
         I will shout over Philistia."

  Who will lead me to the fortified city?
  Who will lead me as far as Edom?

O God!
Have you rejected us?
You did not march out with our army!

O God!
Give us help against the enemy,
    because human help is useless.
I will find strength in God,
    for he will trample on our foes.

Psalm 109

To the Choir Director. A Psalm of David.

He Cries for Help against the Slanders of His Foes

   O God!
     (whom I praise)
   Do not be silent!
   For the mouths of wicked and deceitful people are opened against me;
     They speak against me with lying tongues.
     They surround me with hate-filled words,
     They attack me for no reason.

   Instead of receiving my love,
     they accuse me,
   though I continue in prayer for them.
     They devise evil against me instead of good,
     They devise hatred in place of my love.

   Appoint an evil person over him.
     May an accuser stand at his right side.

   When he is judged:
     May he be found guilty.
     May his prayer be regarded as sin.
     May his days be few.
     May another take over his position.
     May his children become fatherless.
     May his wife become a widow.
     May his children roam around begging,
      seeking food while driven far from their ruined homes.
     May creditors seize all his possessions.
     May foreigners loot the property he has acquired.

May no one extend gracious love to him.
May no one show favor to his fatherless children.
May his descendants be eliminated.
May their memory be erased from the next generation.
May his ancestors' guilt be remembered before YHWH.
May his mother's guilt not be erased.
May what they have done be continuously before YHWH.
May their memory be excised from the earth.

For-
  He did not think to extend gracious love.
    He harassed to death the poor, the needy, and the broken hearted.
    He loved to curse—
      (May his curses return upon him!)
    He took no delight in blessing others.
      (May blessings be far from him!)
    He wore curses like a garment:
      (May they enter his soul like water!)
      (May they enter his bones like oil!)
      (May those curses wrap around him like a garment!)
      (May those curses be like a belt that one always wears!)

May this be the way YHWH repays my accusers,
  those who speak evil against me.

Now-
O God, the sovereign Lord!
Defend me for your name's sake!

Because your gracious love is good,
Deliver me!
Indeed-
  I am poor and needy.
  My heart is wounded within me.

I am fading away like a shadow late in the day.
I am shaken off like a locust.
My knees give way from fasting.
My skin is lean, deprived of oil.
I have become an object of derision to them—
  they shake their heads whenever they see me.

Help me!
O sovereign Lord my God!
Deliver me according to your gracious love!
Then they will realize that your hand is in this—
that you,
O YHWH,
have accomplished it.

They will curse,
But- you will bless.
When they attack,
   they will be humiliated,
      while your servant rejoices.

May my accusers be clothed with shame.
May my accusers be wrapped in their humiliation as with a robe.

I will give many thanks to YHWH with my mouth,
   praising him publicly,
for he stands at the right hand of the needy one,
   to deliver him from his accusers.

Psalm 110

A Psalm of David

A declaration from YHWH to my sovereign Lord:
  "Sit at my right hand until
    I make your enemies your footstool."

When YHWH extends your mighty scepter from Zion,
  rule in the midst of your enemies.
Your soldiers are willing volunteers on your day of battle;
  in majestic holiness,
  from the womb,
  from the dawn.
The dew of your youth belongs to you.

YHWH took an oath and will never recant:
  "You are a priest forever,
    after the manner of Melchizedek."

The sovereign Lord is at your right hand:
  He will utterly destroy kings in the time of his wrath.
  He will execute judgment against the nations,
    filling graves with corpses.
  He will utterly destroy leaders far and wide.
  He will drink from a stream on the way,
    then hold his head high.

Psalm 111

Praise YHWH for his mighty Deeds

    Hallelujah!

א	I will give thanks to YHWH with all of my heart
ב	in the assembled congregation of the upright.
ג	Great are the acts of YHWH;
ד	they are within reach of all who desire them.
ה	Splendid and glorious are his awesome deeds,
ו	his righteousness endures forever.
ז	He is remembered for his awesome deeds;
ח	YHWH is gracious and compassionate.
ט	He prepares food for those who fear him;
י	he is ever mindful of his covenant.
כ	He revealed his mighty deeds to his people
ל	by giving them a country of their own.
מ	Whatever he does is reliable and just,
נ	and all his precepts are trustworthy,
ס	sustained through all eternity,
ע	fashioned in both truth and righteousness.
פ	He sent deliverance to his people;
צ	he ordained his covenant to last forever;
ק	his name is holy and awesome.
ר	The fear of YHWH is the beginning of wisdom;
ש	sound understanding belongs to those who practice it.
ת	Praise of God endures forever.

Psalm 112

The Fear of YHWH Brings Blessing

Hallelujah!

א	How happy is the person who fears YHWH,
ב	who truly delights in his commandments.
ג	His descendants will be powerful in the land,
ד	a generation of the upright who will be blessed.
ה	Wealth and riches are in his house,
ו	and his righteousness endures forever.
ז	A light shines in the darkness for the upright,
ח	for the one who is gracious, compassionate, and just.
ט	It is good for the person who lends generously,
י	conducting his affairs with fairness.
כ	He will never be shaken;
ל	the one who is just will always be remembered.
מ	He need not fear a bad report,
נ	for his heart is unshaken, since he trusts in YHWH.
ס	His heart is steadfast, he will not fear.
ע	In the end he will look in triumph over his enemy.
פ	He gives generously to the poor;
צ	his righteousness endures forever;
ק	his horn is exalted in honor.
ר	The wicked person sees this and flies into a rage;
ש	his teeth gnash and wear away.
ת	The desire of the wicked will amount to nothing.

Psalm 113

Praise to the Loving God

Hallelujah!

Give praise!
O you servants of YHWH.
Praise the name of YHWH!

May the name of YHWH be blessed from now to eternity.
May the name of YHWH be praised from the rising to the setting of the sun,
YHWH is exalted high above all the nations;
    his glory beyond the heavens.

Who is like YHWH our God?
    Enthroned in sovereignty on high?
Yet-
    stooping low to observe the sky and the earth?

He lifts the poor person from the dust,
    raising the needy from the trash pile;
        giving him a seat among nobles,
            with the nobles of his people.

He makes the barren woman among her household-
    a happy mother of joyful children.

Hallelujah!

Psalm 114

YHWH's Deliverance of Israel from Egypt

When Israel came out of Egypt,
    the household of Jacob came out from a people of foreign speech.
Judah became his sanctuary,
    Israel his place of dominion.

The Red Sea saw this and fled;
The Jordan River ran backwards;
The mountains skipped like rams;
The hills like lambs.

What happened to you,
    O sea, that you fled?
    O Jordan, that you ran backwards?
    O Mountains, that you skipped like rams?
    O hills, that you skipped like lambs?

Tremble then!
O earth,
  at the presence of YHWH,
  at the presence of the God of Jacob,
    who turned:
      the rock into a pool of water,
      the flinty rock into flowing springs.

Psalm 115

The Idols are False gods

Not to us,
  O YHWH!
Not to us,
  But-
    to your name be given glory
      because of your gracious love and faithfulness.

Why should the heathen nations ask,
    "Where now is their God?"
When our God is enthroned in the heavens?
When he does whatever he desires?

Their idols are made of silver and gold.
They are made by human hands:
    They have mouths,
      but cannot speak;
    They have eyes,
      but cannot see.
    They have ears,
      but cannot hear;
    They have noses,
      but cannot smell;
    They have hands,
      but cannot touch;
    They have feet,
      but cannot walk;
    They have throats,
      but cannot groan with their throats.

Those who craft them will become like them,
  as will all those who trust in them.

O Israel,
Put your full confidence in YHWH!
He is their helper and shield.

O House of Aaron,
   Put your full confidence in YHWH!
      He is their helper and shield.
You who fear YHWH,
   Put your full confidence in YHWH!
      He is their helper and shield.

YHWH remembers and blesses us.
   He will indeed bless the house of Israel;
   He will bless the house of Aaron.
   He will bless those who fear YHWH,
      both the important and the insignificant together.

May YHWH add to your numbers,
   to you and to your descendants.
May you be blessed by YHWH,
   who made the heavens and the earth.

The highest heavens belong to YHWH,
   but he gave the earth to human beings.
Neither can the dead publicly praise YHWH,
   nor those who go down into silence.
But we will bless YHWH from now to eternity.

Hallelujah!

Psalm 116

YHWH Deliverer Me!

I love YHWH because:
>he has heard my prayer for mercy;
>he listens to me whenever I call.

The ropes of death wound around me.
The anguish of the afterlife came upon me.
I encountered distress and sorrow.
Then I called on the name of YHWH,
>"YHWH, please deliver me!"

YHWH is gracious and righteous.
Our God is compassionate.
YHWH watches over the innocent.

I was brought low-
>But he delivered me.

Return to your resting place,
>O my soul,
for YHWH treated you generously.

Indeed-
>you delivered:
>>my soul from death,
>>my eyes from crying,
>>my feet from stumbling.

I will walk before YHWH in the lands of the living.
I will continue to believe,
>even when I say,
>>"I am greatly afflicted"

and speak hastily,
  "All people are liars!"

What shall I return to YHWH for all his benefits to me?
  I will raise my cup of deliverance.
  I will invoke YHWH's name.
  I will fulfill my vows to YHWH in the presence of all his people.

In the sight of YHWH,
the death of his faithful ones is valued.

O YHWH!
  I am indeed your servant.
  I am your servant.
  I am the son of your handmaid.

Because You have released my bonds:
  I will bring you a thanksgiving offering.
  I will call on the name of YHWH!
  I will fulfill my vows to YHWH
    in the presence of all his people,
    in the courts of YHWH's house,
    in your midst,

  O Jerusalem!

Hallelujah!

Psalm 117

Praise YHWH!

Praise YHWH!
All you nations!

Exalt him!
All you peoples!

For:
    his gracious love is great toward us,
    YHWH's faithfulness is eternal.

Hallelujah!

Psalm 118

O Give Thanks to YHWH

    O give thanks to YHWH!
    For:
        he is good;
        his gracious love is eternal.

    Let Israel now say,
        "His gracious love is eternal."
    Let the house of Aaron now say,
        "His gracious love is eternal."
    Let those who fear YHWH now say,
        "His gracious love is eternal."

    I called on YHWH in my distress:
        "YHWH answered me openly.
        YHWH is with me.
        I will not be afraid.
        What can anyone do to me?"

    With YHWH beside me as my helper,
        I will triumph over those who hate me.

    It is better to put your ultimate confidence in YHWH
        than to trust in people.
    It is better to put your ultimate confidence in YHWH
        than to trust in princes.

    All the nations surrounded me;
    But-
        in the name of YHWH,
        I will defeat them.

They surrounded me.
They are around me;
But-
    in the name of YHWH
    I will defeat them.

They surrounded me like bees;
But-
    they will be extinguished like burning thorns.
    In the name of YHWH I will defeat them.

Indeed you oppressed me so much that I nearly fell,
But-
    YHWH helped me.

YHWH is my strength and protector,
    For-
      he has become my deliverer.

There's exultation for deliverance in the tents of the righteous:
    "The right hand of YHWH is victorious!
    The right hand of YHWH is exalted!
    The right hand of YHWH is victorious!"
But—
    I will not die,
    I will live to recount the deeds of YHWH.

YHWH will discipline me severely,
But-
    he will not deliver me over to die.

Open for me the righteous gates,
    So-
      I may enter through them to give thanks to YHWH.
This is YHWH's gate—
    The righteous will enter through it.

I will praise you
Because:
    you have answered me
    you have become my deliverer.

The stone that the builders rejected
    has become the cornerstone.
This is from YHWH—
    it is awesome in our sight.

This is the day that YHWH has made:
Let us rejoice and be glad in it.

O YHWH!
Deliver us!
O YHWH!
Hurry!
Bring success now!

Blessed is the one who comes in the name of YHWH!
Let us bless you from YHWH's house.
    "YHWH is God—
        He will be our light!"
Bind the festival sacrifice with ropes to the horn at the altar.

You are my God!
I will praise you.

O my God!
I will exalt you.

Give thanks to YHWH,
For:
    he is good;
    his gracious love is eternal.

Psalm 119

David's love of Torah

א *Aleph*
  How blessed are those:
    whose life is blameless,
    who walk in the Torah of YHWH!
  How blessed are those:
    who observe his decrees,
    who seek him with all of their heart,
    who practice no evil;
    who walk in his ways.
  You have commanded concerning your precepts,
    that they be guarded with diligence.
  Oh, that my ways were steadfast,
    so I may keep your statutes.
  Then I will not be ashamed,
    since my eyes will be fixed on all of your commands.
  I will praise you with an upright heart,
    as I learn your righteous decrees.
  I will keep your statutes;
    do not ever abandon me.
ב *Beth*
  How can a young man keep his life clean?
    By ordering it according to your word.
  I have sought you with all of my heart;
    do not let me drift away from your commands.
  I have stored what you have said in my heart,
    so I will not sin against you.
  Blessed are you,
  O YHWH!
  Teach me your statutes.

I have spoken with my lips about all your decrees that you
have announced.
I find joy in the path of your decrees,
as if I owned all kinds of riches.
I will meditate on your precepts,
I will respect your ways.
I am delighted with your statutes;
I will not forget your word.

ג *Gimmel*
Deal kindly with your servant
   so I may live and keep your word.
Open my eyes
   so that I see wonderful things in your Torah.
Since I am a stranger on the earth,
   do not hide your commands from me.
My soul is filled with longing for your decrees all the time.
You rebuke the cursed ones,
   who wander from your commands.
Remove scorn and disrespect from me,
   for I observe your decrees.
Though nobles take their seat and gossip about me,
   your servant will meditate on your statutes.
I take joy in your decrees,
   for they are my counselors.

ד *Daleth*
My soul clings to the dust;
   revive me according to your word.
I talked about my ways:
   "Teach me your statutes."
you have answered me.

Help me understand how your precepts function,
   and I will meditate on your wondrous acts.
I weep because of sorrow;
   fortify me according to your word.

Remove false paths from me;
    and graciously give me your Torah.
I have chosen the faithful way;
    I have firmly placed your ordinances before me.
I cling to your decrees;
    O YHWH!
    do not put me to shame.
I run according to the way of your commands,
    for you enable me to do so.

ה *He*

    Teach me,
    O YHWH!
    The way of your statutes,
        and I will observe them without fail.
    Give me understanding,
        and I will observe your Torah.
            I will keep it with all of my heart.
    Help me live my life by your commands,
        because my joy is in them.
    Turn my heart to your decrees
        and away from unjust gain.
    Turn my eyes away from gazing at worthless things,
        and revive me by your ways.
    Confirm your promise to your servant,
        which is for those who fear you.
    Turn away the shame that I dread,
        because your ordinances are good.
    Oh!
    I long for your precepts;
        revive me through your righteousness.

ו *Vav*

    May your gracious love come to me,
    O YHWH!
    May your salvation come to me,
        just as you said.

Then I can answer the one who insults me,
    for I place my trust in your word.
Never take your truthful words from me,
    For I wait for your ordinances.
Then I will always keep your Torah,
    forever and ever.
I will walk in freedom,
    for I seek your precepts.
Then I will speak of your decrees before kings
    and not be ashamed.
I will take delight in your commands,
    which I love.
I will lift up my hands to your commands,
    which I love.
I will meditate on your statutes.

ז *Zayin*
    Remember what you said to your servant,
        by which you gave me hope.
This is what comforts me in my troubles;
    that what you say revives me.
Even though the arrogant utterly deride me,
    I do not turn away from your Torah.
I have remembered your ancient ordinances,
O YHWH!
I take comfort in them.
I burn with indignation because of the wicked
    who forsake your Torah.
Your statutes are my songs,
    no matter where I make my home.
In the night I remember your name,
O YHWH!
and keep your Torah.
I have made it my personal responsibility
    to keep your precepts.

ח *Cheth*
> YHWH is my inheritance;
> I have given my promise to keep your word.
> I have sought your favor with all of my heart;
> > be gracious to me according to your promise.
> I examined my lifestyle
> > and set my feet in the direction of your decrees.
> I hurried and did not procrastinate
> > to keep your commands.
> Though the ropes of the wicked have ensnared me,
> > I have not forgotten your Torah.
> At midnight I will get up to thank you
> > for your righteous ordinances.
> I am united with all who fear you,
> > and with everyone who keeps your precepts.
> O YHWH!
> The earth overflows with your gracious love!
> Teach me your statutes.

ט *Teth*
> O YHWH!
> You have dealt well with your servant,
> > according to your word.
> Teach me both knowledge and appropriate discretion,
> > because I believe in your commands.
> Before I was humbled,
> > I wandered away,
> > > but now I observe your words.
> O YHWH!
> You are good,
> > and do what is good;
> Teach me your statutes.
> The arrogant have accused me falsely;
> > but I will observe your precepts wholeheartedly.
> Their minds are clogged as with greasy fat,
> > but I find joy in your Torah.

It was for my good that I was humbled;
    so that I would learn your statutes.
Torah that comes from you is better for me
    than thousands of gold and silver coins.

י *Yod*
  Your hands made and formed me.
  Give me understanding,
    that I may learn your commands.
  May those who fear you see me and be glad,
    for I have hoped in your word.
  I know,
  O YHWH!
  Your decrees are just,
  You have rightfully humbled me.
  May your gracious love comfort me
    in accordance with your promise to your servant.
  May your mercies come to me that I may live,
    for your Torah is my delight.
  May the arrogant become ashamed,
    because they have subverted me with deceit;
  but as for me,
    I will meditate on your precepts.
  May those who fear you turn to me,
    along with those who know your decrees.
  May my heart be blameless with respect to your statutes
    so that I may not become ashamed.

כ *Kaf*
  I long for your deliverance;
  I have looked to your word,
    placing my hope in it.
  My eyes grow weary
    with respect to what you have promised—
  I keep asking,
    "When will you comfort me?"

Though I have become as dry as a water bag dried by smoke,
>   I have not forgotten your statutes.
How many days must your servant endure this?
When will you judge those who persecute me?
The arrogant have dug pitfalls for me,
>   disobeying your Torah.
All of your commands are reliable.
>   I am persecuted without cause—
Help me!
Though the arrogant nearly destroyed me on earth,
>   I did not abandon your precepts.
Revive me according to your gracious love;
>   and I will keep the decrees that you have proclaimed.

ל *Lamed*

Your word is forever,
O YHWH!
It is firmly established in heaven.
Your faithfulness continues from generation to generation.
You established the earth,
>   and it stands firm.
To this day they stand by means of your rulings,
>   for all things serve you.
Had your Torah not been my pleasure,
>   I would have died in my affliction.
I will never forget your precepts,
>   for you have revived me with them.
I am yours,
Save me!
I have sought your precepts.
The wicked lay in wait to destroy me,
>   while I ponder your decrees.
I have observed that all things have their limit,
>   but your commandment is very broad.

מ *Mem*

O, how I love your Torah!
Every day it is my meditation.
Your commands make me wiser than my adversaries,
    since they are always with me.
I am more insightful than my teachers,
    because your decrees are my meditations.
I have more understanding than the elders,
    for I observe your precepts.
I keep away from every evil choice
    so that I may keep your word.
I do not avoid your judgments,
    for you pointed them out to me.
How pleasing is what you have to say to me—
    tasting better than honey.
I obtain understanding from your precepts;
    therefore I hate every false way.

נ *Nun*

Your Word is a lamp for my feet,
    a Light for my pathway.
I have given my word and affirmed it,
    to keep your righteous judgments.
I am severely afflicted.
Revive me!
O YHWH!
According to your word.
O YHWH!
Accept my voluntary offerings of praise;
Teach me your judgments.
Though I constantly take my life in my hands,
    I do not forget your Torah.
Though the wicked lay a trap for me,
    I have not wandered away from your precepts.
I have inherited your decrees forever,
    because they are the joy of my heart.

    As a result,
    I am determined
        to carry out your statutes forever.
ס *Samek*
    I despise the double-minded,
        but I love your Torah.
    You are my fortress and shield;
    I hope in your word.
    Leave me,
        you who practice evil,
            that I may observe the commands of my God.
    Keep me safe!
      O God!
    As you have promised,
        I will live.
    Do not let me be ashamed of my hope.

    Support me!
        that I may be saved,
            and I will carry out your statutes consistently.
    You reject all who wander from your statutes,
        since their deceitfulness is vain.
    You remove all the wicked of the earth like dross;
        therefore I love your decrees.
    My flesh trembles out of fear of you,
        and I am in awe of your judgments.
ע *Ayin*
    I have acted with justice and righteousness;
        do not abandon me to my oppressors.
    Back up your servant in a positive way;
        do not let the arrogant oppress me.
    My eyes fail as I look for:
        your salvation,
        your righteous promise.

Act toward your servant consistent with your gracious love,
    and teach me your statutes.
Since I am your servant,
    give me understanding,
        so I will know your decrees.
It is time for YHWH to act,
    since they have violated your Torah.
I truly love your commands more than gold,
    including fine gold.
I truly consider all of your precepts—all of them—to be just,
    while I despise every false way.

פ *Peyh*
    Your decrees are wonderful—
        That is why I observe them.
    The disclosure of your words illuminates,
        providing understanding to the simple.
    I open my mouth and pant
        as I long for your commands.
    Turn in my direction!
    Show mercy to me!
        as you have decreed regarding those who love your name.
    Direct my footsteps by your promise;
    Do not let any kind of iniquity rule over me.
    Deliver me from human oppression,
    I will keep your precepts.
    Show favor to your servant,
    Teach me your statutes.
    My eyes shed rivers of tears,
        when others do not obey your Torah.

צ *Tsade*
    O YHWH!
    You are righteous!
    Your judgments are right!
    You have ordered your decrees to us rightly,
        they are very faithful.

My zeal consumes me,
    because my enemies forget your words.
Your word is very pure.
Your servant loves it.
Though I may be small and despised,
    I do not neglect your precepts.
Your righteousness is an eternal righteousness.
Your Torah is true.
Though trouble and anguish overwhelm me,
    your commands remain my delight.
Your righteous decrees are eternal;
    give me understanding,
        and I will live.

ק *Qof*

I have cried out with all of my heart.
    "Answer me,"
O YHWH!
I will observe your statutes.
I have called out to you,
    "Save me so I may keep your decrees."
I get up before dawn and cry for help;
I place my hope in your word.
I look forward to the night watches,
    when I may meditate on what you have said.
Hear my voice according to your gracious love.
O YHWH!
Revive me in keeping with your justice.
Those who pursue wickedness draw near;
    they remain far from your Torah.
But- you are near,
O YHWH!
All of your commands are true.
I discovered long ago about your decrees,
    that you have confirmed them forever.

ר *Resh*
> Look on my misery!
> Rescue me,
>> for I do not ignore your Torah.
> Defend my case!
> Redeem me!
> Revive me according to your promise!
> Deliverance remains remote from the wicked,
>> for they do not seek your statutes.
> Your mercies are magnificent,
> O YHWH!
> Revive me according to your judgments!
> Though my persecutors and adversaries are numerous,
>> I do not turn aside from your decrees.
>>> I watch the treacherous, and despise them,
>>>> because they do not do what you have said.
> Look how I love your precepts.
> O YHWH!
> Revive me according to your gracious love!
> The sum of your word is truth,
>> each righteous ordinance of yours is everlasting.

שׂ/שׁ *Sin/Shin*
> Though nobles persecute me for no reason,
>> my heart stands in awe of your words.
> I find joy at what you have said
>> like one who has discovered a great treasure.
> I despise and hate falsehood,
>> But- I love your Torah.
> I praise you seven times a day
>> because of your righteous ordinances.
> Great peace belongs to those who love your Torah,
>> nothing makes them stumble.
> I am looking in hope for your deliverance,
> O YHWH!
>> as I carry out your commands.

My soul treasures your decrees,
    I love them deeply.
I keep your precepts and your decrees
    because all of my ways are before you.

ת *Tav*
May my cry arise before you,
O YHWH!
Give me understanding according to your Word.
Let my request come before you;
Deliver me!
    as you have promised.
May my lips utter praise,
    for you teach me your statutes.
May my tongue sing about your promise,
    for all of your commands are just.
May your hand stand ready to assist me,
    for I have chosen your precepts.
I am longing for your deliverance
O YHWH!
    For your Torah is my joy.
Let me live,
    and I will praise you;
Let your ordinances help me.
I have wandered away like a lost sheep;
Find your servant,
    for I do not forget your commands.

Psalm 120

The First Song of Ascent

The Fate of All Slanderers

>I cried to YHWH in my distress,
>>and he responded to me.
>>>"O YHWH!
>>>>Deliver me from lips that lie.
>>>>Deliver me from tongues that deceive."
>>>>>What will be given to you?
>>>>>What will be done to you?
>>>>>O treacherous tongue?"
>
>Like a sharp arrow from a warrior,
>>along with fiery coals from juniper trees!
>
>How terrible for me that:
>>I am an alien in Meshech,
>>I reside among the tents of Kedar!
>>I have resided too long with those who hate peace.
>>I am in favor of peace;
>>But-
>>>when I speak peace,
>>>they are in favor of war!

Psalm 121

Second Song of Ascent

Our Help Comes from YHWH

> I lift up my eyes toward the mountains—
> > from where will my help come?
> My help is from YHWH,
> > The Maker of heaven and earth.
>
> He will never let your foot slip,
> > nor will your guardian become drowsy.
>
> Look!
> The one who is guarding Israel,
> > never sleeps,
> > > he does not take naps.
>
> YHWH is your guardian;
> YHWH is your shade at your right side.
>
> The sun will not ravage you by day,
> > nor the moon by night.
>
> YHWH will protect you from all evil,
> > preserving your life.
> YHWH will guard your goings and comings,
> > from this time on and forever.

Psalm 122

The Third Song of Ascent

    I rejoiced when they kept on asking me,
        "Let us go to YHWH's temple."
    Our feet are standing inside your gates,
    O Jerusalem!

    Jerusalem is built,
        a city knitted together.
    To it the tribes ascend—
        the tribes of YHWH—
    as decreed to Israel:
        to give thanks to the name of YHWH.
    Thrones are established there for judgment,
        thrones of the house of David.

    Pray for the peace for Jerusalem:
        "May those who love you be at peace!
        May peace be within your ramparts,
        May prosperity within your fortresses."

    For the sake of my relatives and friends I will now say,
        "May there be peace within you."

    For the sake of the temple of YHWH our God I will now say,
        "I will seek your welfare."

Psalm 123

The Fourth Song of Ascent

To You,
   who sits enthroned in heaven,
I lift up my eyes.

Consider this:
   as the eyes of a servant focus on what his master provides,
   as the eyes of a female servant focus on what her mistress provides,
So our eyes focus on YHWH our God until he has mercy on us.

Have mercy on us!
O YHWH!
Have mercy on us!
   for we have had more than enough of contempt.
Our lives overflow:
   with scorn from those who live at ease,
   with contempt from those who are proud.

Psalm 124

The Fifth Song of Ascent

"If YHWH had not been on our side—"
  let Israel now say,
"If YHWH had not been on our side,
  when men came against us,
  then they would have devoured us alive,
  when their anger burned against us;
  then the flood waters would have overwhelmed us,
  then the torrent would have flooded over us;
  then the swollen waters would have swept us away."

Blessed be YHWH,
  who did not give us as prey to their teeth.
We have escaped like a bird from the hunter's trap.
The snare has been broken!
We have escaped!

Our help is in the name of YHWH,
  the Maker of heaven and earth.

Psalm 125

The Sixth Song of Ascent

Those who are trusting in YHWH
 are like Mount Zion,
  which cannot be overthrown.
They remain forever.
Just as mountains encircle Jerusalem,
 so YHWH encircles his people,
  from now to eternity.
For a scepter of evil will not rest on the land that has been
 allotted to the righteous,
so the righteous will not direct themselves to do wrong.

O YHWH!
Do good to those who are good,
Do good to those who are upright in heart.

But-
for those who choose their own devious paths,
 YHWH will lead them away,
  along with those who practice evil.

Peace be upon Israel!

Psalm 126

The Seventh Song of Ascent

When YHWH brought back Zion's exiles,
  we were like dreamers.
Then our mouths were filled with laughter,
Then our tongues formed joyful shouts.
Then it was said among the nations,
  "YHWH has done great things for them."
The great things that YHWH has done for us gladden us.

Restore our exiles!
O YHWH!
Like the streams of the Negev.

Those who weep while they plant will sing for joy while they harvest.
The one who goes out weeping,
  carrying a bag of seeds,
will surely return with a joyful song,
  bringing in the sheaves from his harvest.

Psalm 127

The Eighth Song of Ascent, by King Solomon

Unless YHWH builds the house,
    its builders labor uselessly.
Unless YHWH guards the city,
    its guards keep watch uselessly.
It is useless:
    to get up early,
    to stay up late,
    to eat the food of exhausting labor.
Truly he gives sleep to those he loves.

Children are a gift from YHWH;
    a productive womb,
        is YHWH's reward.
As arrows in the hand of a warrior,
    so also are children born during one's youth.
How blessed is the man whose quiver is full of them!
    He will not be ashamed
        as they confront their enemies at the city gate.

Psalm 128

The Ninth Song of Ascent

How blessed are all those who fear YHWH,
Since they follow his ways.

You will eat from the work of your hands;
You will be happy,
It will go well for you.
Your wife will be like a fruitful vine within your house;
Your children like olive shoots surrounding your table.

See how the man will be blessed who fears YHWH.

May YHWH bless you from Zion,
May you observe the prosperity of Jerusalem every day that you live!
May you see your children's children!

May peace be on Israel!

Psalm 129

The Tenth Song of Ascent

"Since my youth they have often persecuted me,"
    let Israel repeat it.
"Since my youth they have often persecuted me,
    Yet they never defeated me."

Wicked people ploughed over my back,
    creating long-lasting wounds."

YHWH is righteous—
    he has cut me free from the cords of the wicked.

May all who hate Zion be turned away and be put to shame.
May they become like grass on a roof top,
    that withers before it takes root—
        not enough to fill one's hand
        not enough to bundle in one's arms.
And may those who pass by never tell them,
    "May YHWH's blessing be upon you.
    We bless you in the name of YHWH."

Psalm 130

The Eleventh Song of Ascent

I cry to you from the depths of my soul,
O YHWH!
Listen to my voice!
Let your ears pay attention to what I ask of you!
O sovereign Lord!

If you were to record iniquities,
O sovereign Lord!
Who could stand in your presence?
But-
    with you there is forgiveness,
        that you may be feared.

I wait for YHWH;
My soul waits,
    because I will hope in his word.

My soul looks to the sovereign Lord
    more than watchmen look for the morning;
    indeed-
    more than watchmen for the morning.

O Israel,
Put your ultimate confidence in YHWH!
For with YHWH there is gracious love,
    along with abundant redemption.
He will redeem Israel from all its sins.

Psalm 131

The Twelfth Song of Ascent, by King David

O YHWH!
My heart is not arrogant,
   I do not look haughty.
   I do not aspire to great things,
   I do not concern myself with things beyond my ability.

Instead-
I have composed and quieted myself like a weaned child with its mother;
I am like a weaned child.

Place your ultimate confidence in YHWH,
O Israel,
both now and forever.

Psalm 132

The Thirteenth Song of Ascent

O YHWH!
Remember in David's favor all of his troubles;
How he swore an oath to YHWH,
    vowing to the Mighty One of Jacob,
        "I will not enter my house,
        or lie down on my bed,
        or let myself go to sleep
        or even take a nap,
        until I locate a place for YHWH,
        a dwelling place for the Mighty One of Jacob."

We heard about it in Ephrata;
We found it in the fields of Jaar.
Let us go to his dwelling place,
Let us worship at his footstool.

Arise!
O YHWH!
Go to your resting place,
You and the ark of your strength.

May your priests be clothed with righteousness
May your godly ones shout for joy.
For the sake of your servant David,
    Do not turn away the face of your anointed one.

YHWH made an oath to David from which he will not retreat:
    "One of your sons,
      I will set in place on your throne.
      If your sons keep my covenant,
      If they keep my statutes that I will teach them,
        then their sons will also sit on your throne forever."

For YHWH has chosen Zion, desiring it as his dwelling place.
   "This is my resting place forever.
   Here I will live,
      because I desire to do so:
   I will bless its provisions abundantly;
   I will satisfy its poor with food.
   I will clothe its priests with salvation
   I will clothe its godly ones with shouts of joy.
   I will create a power base for David.
   I have prepared a lamp for my anointed one.
   I will clothe his enemies with disgrace,
   I will put on him a shiny crown."

Psalm 133

The Fourteenth Song of Ascent, by King David

Look how good and how pleasant it is when brothers live together in unity!
It is like precious oil on the head,
    descending to the beard,
      (even to Aaron's beard)
    flowing down to the edge of his robes.
It is like the dew of Hermon
    falling on Zion's mountains.
For there YHWH commanded his blessing—
    Even life everlasting.

Psalm 134

The Fifteenth Song of Ascent

> Bless YHWH!
> All you servants of YHWH,
> > who serve nightly in YHWH's temple.
> Lift up your hands to the holy place,
> > and bless YHWH.
>
> May YHWH, who sustains heaven and earth,
> > bless you from Zion.

Psalm 135

Hallelujah!

  Praise the name of YHWH!
  Give praise!
  You servants of YHWH,
     who are standing in YHWH's temple,
     who are standing in the courtyards of the house of our God.

  Praise YHWH!
     For- YHWH is good
  Sing to his name!
     For- he is gracious.

  It is Jacob- whom YHWH chose for himself;
  It is Israel- whom YHWH chose as his personal possession.
  Indeed-
     I know that YHWH is great,
     I know that our YHWH surpasses all gods.
     I know YHWH does whatever pleases him
        in heaven and on earth,
        in the seas and all its deep regions.
     He makes the clouds rise from the ends of the earth;
        fashioning lightning for the rain,
        bringing the wind from his storehouses.

  It was YHWH who struck down the firstborn of Egypt,
     including both men and animals.
  He sent signs and wonders among you,
  O Egypt,
  before Pharaoh and all his servants.

  He struck down many nations,
     killing many kings—

>   Sihon, king of the Amorites,
>   Og, king of Bashan,
>   every kingdom of Canaan.
> He gave their land as an inheritance,
>   an inheritance to his people Israel.

Your name,
O YHWH!
exists forever.

Your reputation,
O YHWH!
exists throughout the ages.

For—
>   YHWH will vindicate his people,
>   he will show compassion on his servants.

The idols of the nations are made of silver and gold,
created by human hands:
>   Mouths are attributed to them,
>   but they cannot speak;
>   Eyes are attributed to them,
>   but they cannot see;
>   Ears are attributed to them,
>   but they do not hear,
>   Mouths are attributed to them,
>   But there is no breath in them!

Those who craft them—
   (and all who trust in them)
will become like them.

House of Israel,
   bless YHWH!

House of Aaron,
   bless YHWH!

House of Levi,
   bless YHWH!

You who fear YHWH,
   bless YHWH!

Blessed be YHWH from Zion,
   He who lives in Jerusalem.

Hallelujah!

Psalm 136

Give thanks to YHWH,
For-
    he is good,
    his gracious love is everlasting.

Give thanks to the God of gods,
For-
    his gracious love is everlasting.

Give thanks to the sovereign Lord of lords,
For-
    his gracious love is everlasting.

To the one who alone does great and wondrous things,
For-
    his gracious love is everlasting.

To the one who by wisdom made the heavens,
For-
    his gracious love is everlasting.

To the one who spread out the earth over the waters,
For-
    his gracious love is everlasting.

To the one who made the great lights,
For-
    his gracious love is everlasting.

To the one who made the sun to illumine the day,
For-
    his gracious love is everlasting.

To the one who made the moon and stars to illumine the night,
For-
   his gracious love is everlasting.

To the one who struck the firstborn of Egypt,
For-
   his gracious love is everlasting.

To the one who brought Israel out from among them,
For-
   his gracious love is everlasting.

To the one with a strong hand and an active arm,
For-
   his gracious love is everlasting.

To the one who split the Red Sea in two
For-
   his gracious love is everlasting.

To the one who made Israel pass through the middle of it,
For-
   his gracious love is everlasting.

To the one who cast Pharaoh and his armies into the Red Sea,
For-
   his gracious love is everlasting.

To the one who led his people into the wilderness,
For-
   his gracious love is everlasting.

To the one who struck down great kings,
For-
   his gracious love is everlasting.

To the one who killed famous kings,
For-
   his gracious love is everlasting.

Including Sihon, king of the Amorites,
For-
   his gracious love is everlasting.

Including Og, king of Bashan,
For-
   his gracious love is everlasting.

To the one who gave their land as an inheritance,
For-
   his gracious love is everlasting.

To Israel his servant as a possession,
For-
   his gracious love is everlasting.

He it is who remembered us in our lowly circumstances,
For-
   his gracious love is everlasting.

And rescued us from our enemies,
For-
   his gracious love is everlasting.

He gives food to all creatures,
For-
   his gracious love is everlasting.

Give thanks to the God of Heaven,
For- his gracious love is everlasting.

Psalm 137

A Prayer When Israel Was in Exile in Babylon

We sat down and cried by the rivers of Babylon,
    as we remembered Zion.
On the willows we hung our harps,
For- it was there that:
    our captors asked us for songs,
    our torturers demanded joy from us,
        "Sing us one of the songs about Zion!"
How are we to sing the song of YHWH on foreign soil?

If I forget you,
O Jerusalem!
May my right hand cease to function.
May my tongue stick to the roof of my mouth-
    if I do not remember you,
    if I do not consider Jerusalem to be more important than
    my highest joy.

Remember the day of Jerusalem's fall,
O YHWH!
Because of the Edomites who kept saying,
    "Tear it down!
        Tear it right down to its foundations!"
Daughter of Babylon!
You destroyer!

How blessed will be the one who pays you back for what you have done
to us.
How blessed will be the one who seizes your young children
    and dashes them against the wall!

Psalm 138

O YHWH!

I thank you with all of my heart;
    because you heard my words,
I will sing your praise before the heavenly beings.
I will bow down in worship toward your holy temple
I will give thanks to your name for your gracious love and truth,
For- you have done great things to carry out your word
    consistent with your name.
When I called out,
    you answered me;
    you strengthened me.

O YHWH!
All the kings of the earth will give you thanks,
    For- they have heard what you have spoken.
They will sing about the ways of YHWH,
    For- great is the glory of YHWH!
Though YHWH is highly exalted,
Yet-
    he pays attention to those who are lowly regarded,
    he is aware of the arrogant from afar.

Though I walk straight into trouble,
    you will preserve my life,
        stretching out your hand to fight the vehemence of my
        enemies.
        Your right hand will deliver me.
YHWH will complete his purpose is for me.

O YHWH!
Your gracious love is eternal!
Do not abandon the sovereign work of your hand!

Psalm 139

To the Choir Director: A Song of David

   O YHWH!
You have examined me;
You have known me.
You know when I sit down.
You know when I stand up.
You understand what I am thinking when I am distant from you.
You scrutinize my life and my rest;
You are familiar with all of my ways.
Even before I have formed a word with my tongue,
You,
  O YHWH,
know it completely!

You encircle me from back to front,
    placing your hand upon me.

Knowledge like this is too wonderful for me.
    It is beyond my reach.
        I cannot fathom it.

Where can I flee from your spirit?
Where shall I run from your presence?

If I rise to heaven,
   there you are!
If I lay down to rest in the afterlife,
   there you are!
If I take wings with the dawn and settle down on the western horizon:
   your hand will guide me there,
   your right hand will keep a firm grip on me.

If I say,
    "Darkness will surely conceal me,
        the light around me will become night,"
Even the darkness is not dark to you,
    darkness and light are the same to you.

It was you who formed my internal organs,
    fashioning me within my mother's womb.
I praise you,
    because you are fearful and wondrous!
Your work is wonderful,
    I am fully aware of it.

My frame was not hidden from you while I was being crafted in a hidden place,
    knit together in the depths of the earth.
Your eyes looked upon my embryo,
    everything was recorded in your book.
The days scheduled for my formation were inscribed,
    even though not one of them had come yet.

How deep are your thoughts!
O God!
How great is their number!
If I tried to count them,
    they would number more than the sand.
When I awake,
    I will be with you.

O God!
If only you would execute the wicked,
    so that the men guilty of bloodshed would get away from me,
        those who speak against you with evil motives,
        your enemies who are acting in vain.

Do I not hate those who hate you,
  O YHWH!
Don't I?

I loathe those who rebel against you, do I not?
  With consummate hatred I hate them;
    I consider them my enemies too.

O God!
Examine me!
Understand my heart!

Examine me!
Understand my anxious thoughts!

See if there is any wickedness in me,
Then lead me in the eternal way.

Psalm 140

To the Choir Director: A song of David

O YHWH!
Deliver me from evil people!
Preserve me from violent men:
    who craft evil plans in their minds inciting wars every day.
    who sharpen their tongues like a serpent,
      the venom of vipers is on their lips

Musical Interlude

O YHWH!
Protect me from the control of evil people,
Protect me from violent men who have planned to trip me up,
Protect me from the arrogant who:
    have laid a trap for me.
    have spread a net with ropes,
      lining it with snares along the way.

Musical Interlude

So I said to YHWH,
    "You are my God!
    Listen to my voice as I plead for mercy,
      O YHWH!"
O YHWH!
My YHWH!
My strong deliverer!
You have protected my head in the time of battle.
Never grant,
O YHWH,
the desires of the wicked.

Never condone their plans,
so they should not exalt themselves.

Musical Interlude

> May those who surround me discover that the trouble they talk about falls on their own head!
> May burning coals fall on them;
> May they be cast into fire,
> May they be cast into miry pits, never to rise again.
>
> Let not the slanderer become established in the land.
> May evil quickly hunt down the violent man.
>
> I know that YHWH will act on behalf of the tormented,
>> providing justice for the needy.
>
> Surely the righteous will give thanks to your name,
>> while the upright live in your presence.

Psalm 141

A song of David

  O YHWH!
  I cry out to you!
  Be quick to listen to me when I cry out!

  May my prayer be like incense offered before you.
  May my uplifted hands be like the evening sacrifice.

  O YHWH!
  Set a guard over my mouth.
  Keep watch over the door to my lips.
  Do not let my heart turn toward evil.
  Do not let my heart involve itself in wicked activities with men who practice iniquity.
  Do not let me feast on their delicacies.

  Let one who is truly righteous discipline me in gracious love and rebuke me;
     it will be oil for my head,
     do not let my head refuse it.

  My prayers shall continually be against the deeds of wicked people.
     When their judges are thrown off the cliff,
       the people will hear my words,
         for they are appropriate.

  Just as one plows and breaks up the earth,
     our bones are scattered near the entrance to the afterlife.
  Nevertheless-
   my eyes are on you,
     O Sovereign Lord YHWH!

As I seek protection in you,
    Do not leave me defenseless!

Protect me from the trap laid for me,
Protect me from the snares of those who practice evil.
Let the wicked fall into their own nets,
    while I safely travel through them.

Psalm 142

A song of David. Composed while he was hiding in a cave from Saul.

My voice cries out to YHWH!
My voice pleads for mercy to YHWH!

I pour out my complaint to him,
    telling him all of my troubles.
        "Though my spirit grows faint within me,
        you are aware of my path.
        Wherever I go,
        they have hidden a trap for me.
        I look to my right and observe,
        no one is concerned about me.
        There is nowhere I can go for refuge,
        and no one cares for me."

So I cry to you,
O YHWH!
Declaring,
    "You are my refuge,
    You are my only treasure while I am on this earth.
    Pay attention to my cry,
        For- I have been brought very low.
    Deliver me from my tormentors,
        For- they are far too strong for me.
    Break me out of this prison,
        For- I can give thanks to your name.
    The righteous will surround me with joy,
        For- you will deal generously with me."

Psalm 143

A song of David

    O YHWH!
    Hear my prayer!

    Pay attention to my request,
      because you are faithful.

    Answer me in your righteousness.

    Do not enter into judgment with your servant,
      For- no living person is righteous in your sight.
      For- those who oppose me are pursuing my life,
        crushing me to the ground,
        making me sit in darkness
        like those who died long ago.

    As a result:
      my spirit is desolate within me,
      my mind within me is appalled.

    I remember the former times.
    I meditate on everything you have done.
    I think about the work of your hands.
    I stretch out my hands toward you,
      longing for you like in a dry desert.

Musical *Interlude*

    O YHWH!
    Answer me quickly,
      because my spirit is failing.
    Do not hide your face from me;
      lest I will become like the dead.

In the morning:
Let me hear of your gracious love,
     For- in you I trust.
Cause me to know the way I should take,
     For- I have set my hope on you.

Deliver me from my enemies!
  O YHWH!
I have taken refuge in you.

Teach me to do your will,
    For- you are my God.
Let your good Spirit lead me on level ground.

For- the sake of your name,
  O YHWH!
Preserve my life!

For-
   you are righteous,
Bring me out of trouble.

Because-
   of your gracious love:
      you will cut off my enemies.
      you will destroy all who oppose me,
     for-
        I am your servant.

Psalm 144

A song of David

>Blessed be YHWH!
>My Rock!
>For-
>>He trains my hands for battle,
>>He trains my fingers for warfare.
>
>He is:
>>my gracious love,
>>my fortress,
>>my strong tower
>>my deliverer,
>>my Shield,
>>the One in whom I find refuge,
>>the One who subdues peoples under me.

O YHWH!
What are human beings that you should care about them?
What is mortal man that you should think about him?

>A human being is like a mere empty breath;
>>his days are like a fading shadow.

O YHWH!
Bow down and see from your heavens!
Descend to us!
Touch the mountains,
   and they will smolder.
Send forth lightning
   and scatter the enemy.
Shoot your arrows at them,
   and confuse them.

Reach down your hand from your high place;
    rescue me and deliver me from mighty waters,
        from the control of foreigners.
Their mouths speak lies.
Their right hand deceives.

O God!
I will sing a new song to you.
I will play to you on a harp of ten strings—
    to you who gives victory to kings,
        rescuing his servant David from cruel swords.

 Rescue me!
 Deliver me from the hand of the heathen,
  whose mouths speak lies,
  whose right hand deceives.

May our sons in their youth be like full-grown plants,
May our daughters be like pillars destined to decorate a
    palace.
May our granaries be filled,
    storing produce in abundance;
May our sheep bring forth thousands,
    even tens of thousands in our fields.
May our cattle grow heavy with young,
    with no damage or loss.
May there be no cry of anguish in our streets!

Happy are the people to whom these things come;
Happy are the people whose God is YHWH.

Psalm 145

A Psalm of David

א	I will speak highly of you,
	my God and my Sovereign King,
	I will bless your name forever and ever.
ב	I will bless you every day.
	I will praise your name forever and ever.
ג	YHWH is great,
	and to be praised highly,
	though his greatness is infinite.
ד	One generation will acclaim your works to the next generation.
	They will describe your mighty actions to the next generation.
ה	I will speak of the glorious splendor of your majesty,
	as well as your awesome deeds.
ו	People will speak about the might of your greet deeds.
	I will announce your greatness.
ז	They will extol the fame of your abundant goodness.
	They will sing out loud about your righteousness.
ח	Gracious and merciful is YHWH,
	slow to become angry,
	overflowing with gracious love.
ט	YHWH is good to everyone.
	His mercies extend to everything he does.
י	O YHWH!
	Everything you have done will praise you,
	Your holy ones will bless you.
כ	They will speak about the glory of your kingdom,
	They will talk about your might,
ל	in order to make known your mighty acts to mankind—
	as well as the majestic splendor of your kingdom.

מ	Your kingdom is an everlasting kingdom.
	Your authority endures from one generation to another.
נ	God is faithful about everything he says.
	God is merciful in everything he does.
ס	YHWH supports everyone who falls.
	He raises up those who are bowed down.
ע	Everyone's eyes are on you,
	as you give them their food in due time.
פ	You open your hand continually,
	and satisfy the desire of every living thing.
צ	YHWH is righteous in all of his ways
	He is graciously loving in all of his activities.
ק	YHWH remains near to all who call out to him,
	to everyone who calls out to him sincerely.
ר	He fulfills the desire of those who fear him,
	hearing their cry and saving them.
ש	YHWH preserves everyone who loves him,
	But- he will destroy all of the wicked.
ת	My mouth will praise YHWH!
	All creatures will bless his holy name forever!

Psalm 146

Hallelujah!
Praise YHWH!

O my soul!
I will praise YHWH as long as I live,
    singing praises to my God while I exist.

Do not look to nobles for help,
    nor to mere human beings -
        who cannot save you.
When they stop breathing,
    they end up in the dirt!
On that very day their evil plans collapse!

Happy is the person whose help is the God of Jacob,
Happy is the person whose hope is in YHWH his God,
    the Sovereign Maker of heaven and earth,
        the seas and everything in them,
            forever the Guardian of truth,
                who brings justice for the oppressed,
                who gives food to the hungry.

YHWH frees the prisoners;
YHWH gives sight to the blind.
YHWH lifts up those who are weighed down.
YHWH loves the righteous.
YHWH stands guard over the stranger;
He supports both widows and orphans.
But-
He makes the path of the wicked slippery.

    YHWH will reign in sovereignty forever,
        your God,

O Zion,
for- all generations!

Hallelujah!

Psalm 147

Hallelujah!
It is good to sing praise to our God.
It is fitting to sing glorious praise.

YHWH rebuilds Jerusalem:
He gathers together the outcasts of Israel.
He heals the brokenhearted,
He binds up their injuries.
He keeps track of the number of stars,
He assigns names to all of them.

Our YHWH is great.
He is rich in power.
His understanding is infinite.

YHWH supports the afflicted,
But- he casts the wicked to the ground.

Sing to YHWH with thanksgiving,
Compose music to our God with the lyre.

He shields the heavens with clouds,
He prepares rain for the earth
He makes the grass grow on the hills.
He gives wild animals their food,
    including the young ravens when they cry.
He takes no delight in the strength of a horse,
He gains no pleasure in the runner's swiftness.
But-
    YHWH is pleased:
    with those who fear him,
    with those who depend on his gracious love.

Glorify YHWH!
  O Jerusalem!

Praise your God!
  O Zion!
  For-
        He has strengthened the bars of your gates,
            blessing your children within you.
        He grants peace within your borders,
            satisfying you with the finest of wheat.
        He sends out his command to the earth,
            making his Word go forth quickly.
        He supplies snow like wool,
            scattering frost like ashes.
        He casts down his ice crystals like bread fragments.
            (Who can endure his freezing cold?)
        He sends out his word,
            melting them.
        He makes his wind blow,
            making the water flow.

He declares his words only to Jacob,
He declares his statutes and decrees only to Israel.

He has not dealt with any other nation like this;
They never knew his decrees.

  Hallelujah!

Psalm 148

Hallelujah!
Praise YHWH from heaven!
Praise him in the highest places!

Praise him!
    All you his angels.

Praise him!
    All his armies.

Praise him!
    Sun and moon.

Praise him!
    All you shining stars.

Praise him!
    You heaven of heavens.
    You waters above the heavens.

Let all things praise the name of YHWH!
For-
    He himself gave the command that they be created.
    He set them in place to last forever and ever;
    He gave the command and will not rescind it.
Praise YHWH!
    You from the earth,
    You creatures of the sea
    All you depths,
    fire, hail, snow, fog, and wind storm that carry out his command,
    mountains and every hill,
    fruit trees and cedars,

    living creatures and livestock,
    insects and flying birds,
    earthly kings and all peoples,
    nobles and all court officials of the earth,
    young men and young women alike,
    along with older people and children.
Let them praise the name of YHWH!
    For-
        His name alone is lifted up;
        His majesty transcends earth and heaven.
        He has raised up a source of strength for his people,
            an object of praise for all of his holy ones,
                that is for the people of Israel who are near him.

            Hallelujah!

Psalm 149

Hallelujah!
O sing a new song to YHWH,
    praising him where the godly gather together.

May Israel rejoice in her Makers,
May Zion's descendants rejoice in their King!
May they praise his name with dancing, singing songs to him
With tambourines and lyres.
For –
    YHWH is pleased with his people,
    He beautifies the afflicted with salvation.

May those he loves be exalted.
May those he loves sing for joy on their couches.

Let the high praises to God be heard in their throats.
Let them wield two-edged swords in their hands as they bring:
    retribution to heathen nations,
    punishment to peoples:
        binding their kings with chains,
        binding their officials with iron bands,
        executing the judgment written against them.
    This is honor for all the ones he loves.

Hallelujah!

Psalm 150

A Psalm for Public Worship

Hallelujah!
Praise God in his holy place.
Praise him in his great expanse.
Praise him for his mighty works.
Praise him according to his excellent greatness.
Praise him with trumpet sounding.
Praise him with stringed instrument and harp.
Praise him with tambourine and dancing.
Praise him with stringed and wind instruments.
Praise him with loud cymbals.
Praise him with reverberating cymbals.
Let everyone who breathes praise YHWH.
Hallelujah!

Appendix A

Philosophy of Translation

In order to enhance the experiential nature of the Psalms, several things had to be done. First, I needed to produce a new dynamic translation of the Psalms from the Hebrew text. My translation goes beyond any other translation for several reasons:

First, I have removed the verse numbering invented centuries ago by someone who did not know any Hebrew whatsoever. While translating the Psalms I constantly found the verse numbering in the way of following the flow of the heart and mind of the Psalmist. The verse numbering often cut the flow of ideas into disjointed sentences.

Second, the King James Version inserted far too much Elizabethan poetry into its translation of the Psalms. My new translation of the Psalms is totally free from previous translations.

Third, I formatted the text to follow the flow of ideas in the mind of the Psalmist. Numerous volunteers (both clergy and laity, male and female, educated and uneducated, etc.) proof read the final version and they discovered they could follow the flow of the thoughts, prayers, worship, and praise of the Psalmist all the way into the very presence of God. They experienced "knee-ology" and not just theology.

Fourth, the divine name YHWH is not mistranslated "LORD" or "Jehovah" but placed in the text as it appears in the Hebrew. YHWH does not have any inspired vowels and thus cannot be pronounced. Borrowing the vowels from Adonai and inserting them into YHWH is where the false name "Jehovah" originated.

YHWH is derived from the Hebrew word for "being" and emphasizes that God was and is and always shall be God. The "emerging" god of Process theology and the "Open View" of God is not the God of the Bible.

The reason I place YHWH in my translation is that the various names of God reveal different aspects of the nature and work of God. YHWH is God's personal name that is used to emphasize the covenantal relationship between God and His elect people. The Psalmist uses YHWH whenever he has in view his personal relationship to the covenant God of Israel.

For example, in Psa. 23, David writes, "YHWH is continuously shepherding me all the time." He used the name YHWH instead of Elohim, Adonai, etc. because he had in mind his personal relationship with God.

The divine name, Adonai, comes from the Hebrew word for pillar and emphasizes the sovereign strength of the God who upholds and holds together the universe. That is why I translate it as "sovereign Lord."

Fifth, I wrote the book, *Death and the Afterlife,* to demonstrate that the Bible teaches a conscious afterlife, and not soul sleep or some other Gentile heresy. The Hebrew word "sheol" was mistranslated as grave and pit by the KJV, and the cults such as the Jehovah's Witnesses have used this error to prove that at death we do not go to heaven or hell, but are unconscious in the grave.

The Hebrew word "sheol" refers to the conscious afterlife and not to the grave or a pit. For this reason I translated it as "the afterlife." For the documentation to support our translation, see Appendix Two.

Sixth, the Western philosophic tradition that divided life into a secular versus sacred dichotomy viewed the word "law" in the Bible in terms of legal case law in the context of the courtroom.

The Western Gentile world knew nothing of the biblical concept of "Torah" that embraced all of life. The biblical authors did not believe in a secular dimension in life. To them YHWH was King over all of life. Every square inch of the earth is YHWH's and the fullness therein.

We have translated various Hebrew words such as "law" as "Torah" to indicate that all of life is to be lived for the glory of God. Psa. 119 takes on a deeper meaning when you understand that David loved the all-embracing Torah.

Too any Gentile readers automatically assume that when David said he loved the "law," he meant the Ten Commandments. This has caused confusion as, who in their right mind, would "love" dry, cold legal codes? No. by "law" David meant the all-embracing Torah of life and blessing.

Seventh, some of the Psalms were arranged to follow the Hebrew alphabet. The KJV only revealed this structure in Psa. 119. We have added the other Psalms that use this memory aid.

Eighth, we have incorporated the latest research on ancient Ugaritic and Akkadian prayers and hymns and other ancient Near Eastern poetry. Amazing insights into biblical literature can be gained from studying it in the light of its historical and cultural context. The Psalms did not drop out of heaven but were created in their respective historical, cultural, and literary context.

One grammatical point is the use of ellipsis. It is literary technique in which, in order to save time and effort, the author assumes that when he is writing a series of things, he can omit repeating the first words because he assumes that the reader will automatically add those words in his mind. The words are not repeated in the text because they are to be supplied by the mind of the reader.

For example, suppose he wants us to praise the Lord in various ways. He begins writing, "Praise the Lord with..." and then lists ways to do this. "Praise the Lord with the harp, lyre, trumpet, dance, drums, song, hymn, etc." He assumes that the reader is smart enough to repeat in his mind the words "Praise the Lord with...". Thus he does not have to write out all those words per se. For example, "Praise the Lord with the harp, the lyre, the trumpet," etc., by ellipsis becomes:

>Praise the Lord with the harp.
>Praise the Lord with the lyre.
>Praise the Lord with trumpet. etc.

I have written out the words that by ellipsis were meant to be understood as part of the text. The enthusiastic response of readers has been beyond my earnest expectation. It opens new levels of meaning for the modern reader.

Ninth, the Hebrew word "vav" (and, or, etc.) is an element of the poetic style of ancient Hebrew poetry that does not translate well into English. Its purpose had more to do with oral recitation than written communication. Modern translators often skip over the vav because it would hinder understanding of the text in English. While consecutive vavs were vocalized as a memory technique, I have not included them in my translation whenever I felt they hindered the clarity of the text.

Tenth, the Hebrew text of the Psalms at times is missing key nouns, verbs, etc. I had to examine the Greek, Latin, and other ancient translations to figure out the original text. Sometimes I repeated words from the previous line that smoothed out the poetry and clarified the thought of the Psalmist. My purpose in this translation is to make clear to the modern reader the very heart and mind of the Psalmists, not to render a wooden literalistic translation that obscures the thoughts of the Psalmists.

Eleventh, since most of the Psalms were composed for vocal or instrumental music, this must be taken into account in translation. This is particularly true for antiphonal singing between the cantor and the choir or congregational, repeating refrains, and musical pauses, etc. Having a background in music theory and composition has helped me immensely to see where these musical structures need to be in the translation.

May God bless your meditation on the Psalms with His own presence. There is no greater good than the smile of God and no greater evil than His frown.

Appendix B

THE MEANING OF SHEOL

One of the most crucial issues that determine our understanding of what the Bible teaches about death and the afterlife is the proper interpretation of such key terms as Sheol. No study of death is complete without a thorough understanding of this Hebrew word.

SHEOL

The Hebrew word Sheol is found 66 times in the Old Testament. While the Old Testament consistently refers to the body as going to the grave, it always refers to the soul or spirit of man as going to Sheol. The nature of Sheol and the condition of those in it is crucial to our understanding of what the Bible teaches about what happens to man after death.

The Lexicographical Material

The first step in understanding any ancient or foreign word is to check the lexicons, dictionaries, encyclopedias, etc., which deal with that language.

Brown, Driver and Briggs based their *A Hebrew and English Lexicon of the Old Testament* on the work of Gesenius, one of the greatest Hebrew scholars who ever lived. They define Sheol as: "the underworld...whither man descends at death" (p. 982.). They trace the origin of Sheol to either *sha-al*, which means the spirit world to which mediums directed their questions to the departed, or *sha-al*, which refers to the hollow place in the earth where the souls of men went at death.

Langenscheidt's *Hebrew/English Dictionary to the Old Testament* (p. 337) defines *Sheol* as: "netherworld, realm of the dead, Hades." *The International Standard Bible Encyclopedia* in Vol. IV, p. 2761, defines Sheol as: "the unseen world, the state or abode of the dead, and is the equivalent of the Greek: Hades." Keil and Delitzsch state that "Sheol denotes the place where departed souls are gathered after death; it is an infinitive form from *sha-al*, to demand, the demanding, applied to the place which inexorably summons all men into its shade." [1]

The lexicographical evidence is so clear that the great Princeton scholar, B. B. Warfield; stated that with Hebrew scholars, there is no...hesitation to allow with all heartiness that Israel from the beginning of its recorded history cherished the most settled conviction of the persistence of the soul in life after death.

> ...The body is laid in the grave and the soul departs to Sheol. [2]

George Eldon Ladd in *The New Bible Dictionary* (p. 380), comments:

> In the Old Testament, man does not cease to exist at death, but his soul descends to Sheol. Modern scholarship understands the word Sheol to refer to the place where the soul or spirit of man goes at death. [3]

> None of the lexicographical literature defines Sheol as referring to the grave or to passing into nonexistence.

Comparative Studies

In order to understand what a certain word meant in an ancient language, it is sometimes helpful to find any parallel words in the other languages of that time. Thus comparative studies of Sheol have been done which demonstrate that Sheol's parallels in other languages meant the place where the soul of man goes at death. No research has found a place where Sheol's parallel means the grave or nonexistence. For example, The Ugaritic *ars* and Accadian *su alu* clearly refer to the netherworld. [4] The Babylonians, Assyrians, Egyptians, and Greek parallels to

Sheol clearly meant the place of departed spirits. [5] The Ethiopian *Si'ol* cannot mean anything other than the netherworld, the place of conscious life after death. [6]

The Historical Context

What is important about comparative studies is that they place biblical words in their historical context. The word Sheol should thus be understood in terms of what it meant in the Hebrew language and by its parallel in the other languages of that time. Why?

When God wanted Israel to believe something which was unique and contrary to what the surrounding cultures believed, He always clearly condemned and forbade the pagan beliefs and then stressed the uniqueness of the new concept. For example, in order to establish monotheism, God repeatedly and clearly condemned the pagan concept of polytheism and stressed monotheism.

While God clearly condemned polytheism in the Old Testament, at no time did He ever condemn belief in a conscious afterlife. At no time did God ever put forth the concept of annihilation or nonexistence as the fate of man's soul at death.

Also, when Israel had a unique and contrary belief, the pagan societies around Israel would use this belief as the grounds to persecute the Jews. Thus the Jews were persecuted for rejecting polytheism and believing in monotheism. Daniel's three friends who were thrown into a fiery furnace are an excellent example of such persecution.

Yet, where in recorded history did pagan religions or societies persecute the Jews because they denied a conscious afterlife? To think that the Jews could go against the universally held concept of a conscious afterlife and that the pagans would not seize upon this as a pretense for persecution is absurd.

Since the universality of belief in a conscious afterlife is irrefutable, and there is no evidence that Israel deviated from this belief, we must assume that the Old Testament taught a conscious afterlife in Sheol as the fate of man's soul or spirit.

The Rabbinic Literature

It is universally recognized by Talmudic scholars that *Sheol* never meant the grave or unconsciousness in rabbinic literature. Ginzburg states that in rabbinic writings one finds a consistent conviction that "there exists after this world a condition of happiness or unhappiness for an individual." [7] Guttman adds,

> "The Talmud, like the Apocryphal literature, knows of a kind of intermediate state of the soul between death and resurrection; true retribution will be dispensed only after the resurrection of the body. But along with this, we also find the fate in a retribution coming immediately after death and in a life of blessedness for the soul in the beyond."[8]

The rabbinic tradition before, during, and after the time of Christ describes the soul departing the body and descending into *Sheol* at death. [9]The rabbis consistently pictured both the righteous and the wicked as conscious after death.[10]

The evidence is so overwhelming that the classic Princeton theologian, Charles Hodge, stated, "That the Jews believed in a conscious life after death is beyond dispute." [11]

The annihilationists have never discovered any evidence that the majority of Jews believed that the soul was extinguished at death. There is no conflict in the rabbinic literature over this issue.[12]

Sheol and the Grave

The KJV translates Sheol as "hell" 31 times, "grave" 31 times, and "pit" three times. Because of this inconsistency of translation, such groups as the Adventists, Armstrongites, and Jehovah's Witnesses have taught that Sheol means the grave.

All the conditional immortalitists have traditionally capitalized on the KJV's translation of Sheol as the "grave." For example, in *The Conditionalist Faith of Our Fathers* (Vol. I, pp. 162 and 298), Froom emphatically stated that both Sheol and Hades meant the grave. It is to be regretted that even some modern versions have carried on the tradition of translating Sheol as grave.

Since the conditional immortalitists stress that Sheol means the grave, we will pause at this point to demonstrate that Sheol *cannot* mean the grave.

First, exegetically speaking, the initial occurrence of Sheol in the Old Testament cannot mean the grave. The word Sheol is first found in Gen. 37:35. After the brothers had sold Joseph into slavery, they informed their father that Joseph had been killed and devoured by a savage beast. As Jacob held the bloodied and tattered remains of Joseph's coat in his hands, he declared:

> A wild beast has devoured him: Joseph has
> surely been torn to pieces. (v. 33)

As a result of the shock of the death of Joseph, Jacob cried:

> Surely I will go down to Sheol in mourning
> for my son. (v. 35, lit. Heb.)

There are several things about this first occurrence of Sheol which should be pointed out.

1. Jacob assumed that his son was still alive and conscious after death and that he would eventually reunite with his son after his own death. The German commentator Lange comments:

> One thing is clear: [Joseph's death] was not a state of nonbeing... Jacob was going to be with his son; he was still his son; there was yet a tie between him and his son; he was still spoken of as a personality; he is still regarded as having a being somehow and somewhere. [13]

2. Whatever else Sheol may mean, in this passage it cannot mean Joseph's grave, for Jacob believed that Joseph had been devoured by an animal and had no grave. Since Joseph had no grave, it is impossible for Jacob to be referring to being buried in a common grave with his son.

3. According to the context, Jacob is clearly speaking of reuniting with his favorite son in the underworld, here called Sheol. He even speaks of "going down" to reunite with his son, because it was assumed that Sheol was the place of departed spirits, probably a hollow place in the center of the earth.

The second reason for not identifying Sheol as the grave is that when the biblical authors wanted to speak of the grave, they used the word *kever*. That they did not view *kever* and Sheol as synonymous is clear from the way these words are used throughout the Old Testament. For example, in Isa. 14:19, the king is cast out of his grave *(kever)* in order to be thrown into Sheol where the departed spirits can rebuke him (vv. 9, 10). In this passage, Sheol and *kever* are opposites, not synonyms.

Third, in the Septuagint, Sheol is never translated as *mneema*, which is the Greek word for grave. It is always translated as Hades which meant the underworld. *Kever* is translated as *mneema* 36 times and as *taphos* 45 times. But *kever* is never translated as Hades just as Sheol is never translated as *mneema*.

Fourth, *kever* and Sheol are never used in Hebrew poetic parallelism as equivalents. They are always contrasted and never equated. *Kever* is the fate of the body, while Sheol is the fate of the soul (Ps. 16:8–11).

Fifth, Sheol is "under the earth," or "the underworld," while graves were built as sepulchres above the earth, or caves, or holes in the earth. Sheol is called the underworld in Isa. 14:9. It is also called "the lower parts of the earth" (KJV) in Ps. 63:9; Isa. 44:23; Ezek. 26:20; 31:14, 16, 18;

32:18, 24. Sheol is the opposite of heaven (Ps. 139:8). One must go "down" to get to Sheol (Gen. 37:35).

Sixth, while bodies are unconscious in the grave, those in Sheol are viewed as being conscious (Isa. 14:4–7; 44:23; Ezek. 31:16; 32:21).

Seventh, an examination of the usages of *kever* and Sheol reveals that Sheol cannot mean the grave. The following twenty contrasts between *kever* and Sheol demonstrates this point:

1. While the *kabar* (to bury) is used in connection with *kever*, it is never used in connection with Sheol. We can bury someone in a grave but we cannot bury anyone in Sheol (Gen. 23:4, 6, 9, 19, 20; 49:30, 31, etc.).

2. While *kever* is found in its plural form "graves" (Ex. 14:11), the word Sheol is never pluralized.

3. While a grave is located at a specific site (Ex. 14:11), Sheol is never localized, because it is everywhere accessible at death no matter where the death takes place. No grave is necessary in order to go to Sheol.

4. While we can purchase or sell a grave (Gen. 23:4–20), Scripture never speaks of Sheol being purchased or sold.

5. While we can own a grave as personal property (Gen. 23:4–20), nowhere in Scripture is Sheol owned by man.

6. While we can discriminate between graves and pick the "choicest site" (Gen. 23:6), nowhere in Scripture is a "choice" Sheol pitted against a "poor" Sheol.

7. While we can drop a dead body into a grave (Gen. 50:13), no one can drop anyone into Sheol.

8. While we can erect a monument over a grave (Gen. 35:20). Sheol is never spoken of as having monuments.

9. While we can, with ease, open or close a grave (2 Kings 23:16), Sheol is never opened or closed by man.

10. While we can touch a grave (Num. 19:18), no one is ever said in Scripture to touch Sheol.

11. While touching a grave brings ceremonial defilement (Num. 19:16), the Scriptures never speak of anyone being defiled by Sheol.

12. While we can enter and leave a tomb or grave (2 Kings 23:16), no one is ever said to enter and then leave Sheol.

13. While we can choose the site of our own grave (Gen. 23:4–9), Sheol is never spoken of as something we can pick and choose.

14. While we can remove or uncover the bodies or bones in a grave (2 Kings 23:16), the Scriptures never speak of man removing or uncovering anything in Sheol.

15. While we can beautify a grave with ornate carvings or pictures (Gen. 35:20), Sheol is never beautified by man.

16. While graves can be robbed or defiled (Jer. 8:1, 2), Sheol is never spoken of as being robbed or defiled by man.

17. While a grave can be destroyed by man (Jer. 8:1, 2), nowhere in Scripture is man said to be able to destroy Sheol.

18. While a grave can be full, Sheol is never full (Prov. 27:20).

19. While we can see a grave, Sheol is always invisible.

20. While we can visit the graves of loved ones, nowhere in Scripture is man said to visit Sheol.

Sheol and Its Inhabitants

Given the Principle of progressive revelation, it is no surprise that the Old Testament is vague in its description of Sheol and the condition of those in it. While the Old Testament prophets stated many things about Sheol, they did not expound in any measure of depth on this subject. Another reason for this vagueness is that a conscious afterlife was so universally accepted that it was assumed by the biblical authors to be the belief of anyone who read the Scriptures. Since it was not a point of conflict, no great attention was given to it.

The following things are stated about Sheol with the caution that figurative language was used by biblical authors in their description of Sheol and the conditions of those in it. Much harm has been done by literalizing what was intended to be figurative.

> First, Sheol is said to have "gates" by which one enters and "bars" which keep one in (Job 17:16; Isa. 38:10). Such figurative language conveys the idea that Sheol is a realm from which no escape is possible.
>
> Second, the Old Testament describes Sheol in the following ways:
>
>> 1. Sheol is a shadowy place or place of darkness (Job 10:21, 22; Ps. 143:3). Evidently, it is another dimension which is not exposed to the rays of the sun.
>>
>> 2. It is viewed as being "down," "beneath the earth," or in "the lower parts of the earth" (Job 11:8; Isa. 44:23; 57:9; Ezek. 26:20; Amos 9:2). These figures of speech should not be literalized into an absurd cosmology. They merely indicate that Sheol is not a part of this world but has an existence of its own in another dimension.
>>
>> 3. It is a place where one can reunite with his ancestors, tribe or people (Gen. 15:15; 25:8; 35:29; 37:35; 49:33; Num. 20:24, 28; 31:2; Deut. 32:50; 34:5; 2 Sam. 12:23). This cannot refer to one common mass grave where everyone was buried.

No such graves ever existed in recorded history. Sheol is the place where the souls of all men go at death. That is why Jacob looked forward to reuniting with Joseph in Sheol. While death meant separation from the living, the Old Testament prophets clearly understood that it also meant reunion with the departed.

4. It seems that Sheol has different sections. There is the contrast between "the lowest part" and "the highest part" of Sheol (Deut. 32:22). This figurative language implies that there are divisions or distinctions within Sheol. Perhaps the Old Testament's emphatic distinction between the righteous and the wicked in this life indicates that this distinction continues on in the afterlife. Thus the wicked are said to be in "the lowest part," while the righteous are in "the higher part" of Sheol. While this is not clearly stated in the Old Testament, there seems to be some kind of distinction within Sheol. Later rabbinic writers clearly taught that Sheol had two sections. The righteous were in bliss in one section while the wicked were in torment in the other.

Third, the condition of those in Sheol is described in the following ways:

1. At death man becomes a *rephaim*, i.e., a "ghost," "shade," or "disembodied spirit" according to Job 26:5; Ps. 88:10; Prov. 2:18; 9:18; 21:16; Isa. 14:9; 26:14, 19. Instead of describing man as passing into nonexistence, the Old Testament states that man becomes a disembodied spirit. The usage of the word *rephaim* irrefutably establishes this truth. Langenscheidt's *Hebrew-English Dictionary to the Old Testament* (p. 324) defines *rephaim* as

referring to the "departed spirits, shades." Brown, Driver and Briggs (p. 952) define *rephaim* as "shades, ghosts...name of dead in Sheol." Keil and Delitzsch define *rephaim* as referring to "those who are bodiless in the state after death."

From the meaning of *rephaim*, it is clear that when the body dies, man enters a new kind of existence and experience. He now exists as a spirit creature and experiences what angels and other disincarnate spirits experience.

Just as angels are disincarnate energy beings composed only of "mind" or mental energy and are capable of supra-dimensional activity and such things as thought and speech without the need of a physical body, even so once man dies, he too becomes a disembodied supra-dimensional energy being and is capable of thought and speech without the need of a body. This is why the dead are described as "spirits" and "ghosts" throughout the Scriptures.

This concept is carried on into the New Testament in such places as Luke 24:37–39. A belief in "ghosts" necessarily entails a belief that man survives the death of the body.

2. Those in Sheol are pictured as conversing with each other and even making moral judgments on the lifestyle of new arrivals (Isa. 14:9–20; 44:23; Ezek. 32:21). They are thus conscious entities while in Sheol.

3. Once in Sheol, all experiences related exclusively to physical life are no longer possible. Those in Sheol do not marry and procreate children because they do not have bodies. Neither do they plan and execute business transactions. Once in Sheol, they cannot attend public worship

in the temple and give sacrifices or praise. There are no bodily pleasures such as eating or drinking. Those in Sheol do not have any wisdom or knowledge about what is happening in the land of the living. They are cut off from the living. They have entered a new dimension of reality with its own kind of existence (Ps. 6:5; Eccles. 9:10, etc.).

4. God's judgment upon the wicked does not cease when the wicked die in their sins. Thus some of the spirits in Sheol experience the following:

> a. God's anger (Deut. 32:22): According to Moses, the wicked experience the fire of YHWH's anger in the "lowest part of Sheol." This passage would make no sense if the wicked are nonexistent and Sheol is the grave.
>
> b. Distress (Ps. 116:3): The Hebrew word *matzar* refers to the distress that is felt when in the straits of a difficulty. It is found in this sense in Ps. 118:5. Also, the word *chevel,* which is the poetic parallel for *matzar,* means "cords of distress" (2 Sam. 22:6; Ps. 18:6).
>
> c. Writhing in pain (Job 26:5): The Hebrew word *chool* means to twist and turn in pain like a woman giving birth.

It is obvious that nonexistence can hardly experience anger, distress, or pain. Thus, there are hints in the above passages that not everyone experiences blessedness in the afterlife. Beyond these three passages, the Old Testament does not speak of torment in the intermediate state. While it speaks of the "everlasting humiliation and contempt" which awaits the wicked after the resurrection (Dan. 12:2), the Old Testament tells us very little about the intermediate suffering of the wicked in Sheol.

5. In the Old Testament, the righteous as well as the wicked went to Sheol at death (Gen. 37:35). Although this is true, the Old Testament saints did not have a clear understanding of what to expect in Sheol. They were constantly torn by mixed emotions when they contemplated their death. They did not experience the same joy and bold confidence that New Testament saints express (Acts 7:59). While New Testament saints think of death as a "gain" (Phil. 1:21), the Old Testament saints thought of it as "loss."

Given the principle of progressive revelation, Old Testament saints simply did not have all the information which was needed to approach death with peace and joy. Just as the lack of New Testament revelation prevented them from obtaining a clear conscience and full assurance of faith (Heb. 10:1–14), even so they could not approach death with joy. That this is true can be established upon several lines of reasoning.

First, the writer to the book of Hebrews tells us that the Old Testament saints were in bondage to the fear of death and that Satan used this to oppress them.

> Since then the children share in flesh and blood, He Himself likewise also partook of the same, that through death He might render powerless him who had the power of death, that is, the devil; and might deliver those who through fear of death were subject to slavery all their lives. (Heb. 2:14, 15)

Only after the Messiah came and wrested the keys of death and Hades from the Evil One would God's people experience freedom from the fear of death (Rev. 1:18).

The bondage of fear which gripped the Old Testament saints expressed itself in different ways. They had a fear of being separated from their living loved ones. They were afraid of being severed from the joys of life (Ps. 6). They begged to be delivered from death and Sheol because they did not look forward to death (Ps. 13). This is why they spoke of the "sorrows" (KJV) and "terrors" of death (Ps. 18:4; 55:4; 116:3) instead of the triumph in death which New Testament saints express (2 Tim. 4:6–8).

Second, while the overall picture of death was somewhat gloomy in the Old Testament, yet God had begun to reveal to His people that they would be ushered into His joyous presence after death. To be sure, these were only hints of glory, but hints they were. The ascension of Enoch and Elijah to heaven indicated that the righteous could be taken into God's presence (Gen. 5:24, cf. Heb. 11:5; 2 Kings 2:11).

The verb which described Enoch's and Elijah's ascension (*laqach*) was later used to describe the passage of the righteous out of Sheol into heaven (Ps. 49:15; cf. 73:24). Asaph expressed the hope that he would go to dwell at the throne of glory at death. Later rabbinic writers consistently spoke of the righteous going to the throne of glory at death.

> Nevertheless I am continually with Thee; Thou hast taken hold of my right hand. With Thy counsel Thou wilt guide me, and afterward *receive me to glory*. Whom have I in heaven but Thee? And besides Thee, I desire nothing on earth. (Ps. 73:23–25)

The Old Testament saints looked forward to reuniting with their departed loved ones (Gen. 37:35). This must have afforded them some comfort.

Also, the Old Testament believers knew that Sheol was open to God's sight (Job 26:6) and that they would still be in God's presence and protection (Ps. 139:8).

Conclusion

While the patriarchs went in mourning to Sheol, by the time of the Wisdom literature, a more optimistic note was beginning to be sounded. The progress from Gen. 37:35 to Ps. 73:24 indicates a gradual change of attitude toward death which progressive revelation made possible. While the early Old Testament saints knew that they were going to Sheol at death, later, believers felt they would be taken to heaven to be at God's throne after death.

FOOTNOTES

[1] Keil & Delitzsch, *Commentaries on the Old Testament*, (Eerdmans, Grand Rapids, n.d.: I:338).

[2] *Select Shorter Wrings of Benjamin Warfield*, (ed. Meeter: P & R, 1970) pgs. 339, 345.

[3] See Charles, Fife, Hough, Motzer, Marcarnty, Tromp, etc.

[4] N. Tromp, *Primitive Conceptions of Death and the Nether World in the Old Testament*, (Rome: Pontifical Biblical Institute, 1969) p.6.

[5] R. Charles, *A Critical History of the Doctrine of a Future Life*, (London: Adam & Charles Block, 19130 pp. 34f.

[6] M. Fisher, "Some Contributions of Ethiopic Studies," in The Law and the Prophets, (NJ: P & R, 1974) p. 81.

[7] *Essays in Greco-Roman and Related Talmudic Literature*, (New York: KTAV Pub. House, 1977) p. 36.

[8] ibid., p. 42.

[9] Midrash: Gen. 96, 908, Tal. Shah 589; 777-779; Enoch 103.7, etc.

[10] Midrash: Gen. 409, 516, Num. 733; Ecc. 83, 229; Bal. Tal.: Shah 777-779; PT Moed Katan 111.5, 826, Yebamuth XVI.3.15c, Bereshith Rabba c. 7, Vayyekin Rabba XVIII.1; Kohelith rabb 1: 15, ed., Rom. 6a; Ruth Rabba 111.3, 6c, etc.

[11] C. Hodge, ST, (London: Clark, 1960) III:770;

[12] *Essays In Greco-Roman and Related Talmudic Literature*, (New York: KTAV Pub. House, 1977), p.p. 43-44.

[13] Keil & Delitsch, ibid, II:52